SCIENCE IN A JAR

SCIENCE
IN A
JAR

35+ Experiments

in Biology, Chemistry, Weather,

the Environment, and More!

JULIA GARSTECKI

Inspiring | Educating | Creating | Entertaining

Brimming with creative inspiration, how-to projects, and useful information to enrich your everyday life, Quarto Knows is a favorite destination for those pursuing their interests and passions. Visit our site and dig deeper with our books into your area of interest: Quarto Creates, Quarto Cooks, Quarto Homes, Quarto Lives, Quarto Drives, Quarto Explores, Quarto Gifts, or Quarto Kids.

© 2019 Quarto Publishing Group USA Inc.

First Published in 2019 by Quarry Books, an imprint of The Quarto Group, 100 Cummings Center, Suite 265-D, Beverly, MA 01915, USA.

T (978) 282-9590 F (978) 283-2742 QuartoKnows.com

Quarry Books titles are also available at discount for retail, wholesale, promotional, and bulk purchase. For details, contact the Special Sales Manager by email at specialsales@quarto.com or by mail at The Quarto Group, Attn: Special Sales Manager, 100 Cummings Center, Suite 265-D, Beverly, MA 01915, USA.

10 9 8 7 6 5 4 3 2 1

ISBN: 978-0-7603-6478-9

Digital edition published in 2019

eISBN: 978-0-7603-6479-6

Library of Congress Cataloging-in-Publication Data available.

Design, Cover Image, and Page Layout: Mattie Wells - mattiewells.com

Photography: Rebeca Wilhile Photography, except pages 8, 10, 12, 25, 31 (left), 33, 36 (right), 50 (right), 58, 62, 73 (bottom), 76, 88, 89 (left), 95 (right), 105 (right), 112 (right), 114, 123, via Shutterstock

Printed in China

TO THE CURIOUS,
WHO NEED TO KNOW WHY

CONTENTS

CHAPTER 1: LIFE SCIENCE

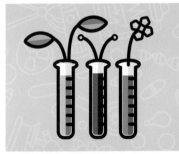

CHAPTER 2: CHEMISTRY

CHAPTER 3: EARTH SCIENCE

CHAPTER 4: PHYSICAL SCIENCE

CHAPTER 5: ENVIRONMENTAL SCIENCE

" No amount of experimentation can ever prove me right; a single experiment can prove me wrong.
—Albert Einstein

INTRODUCTION

The world is full of amazing, beautiful, wonderful, curious things.

Just step outside and take a look. Can you count all the shades of green? How is it possible to see so many different variations of the same color? Notice the sky. What shade is it? Is it cloudy? Clear? Windy or hot?

The whole world is one big science experiment. Everything is something to be investigated!

❯ **Why does your leg look different when you soak your feet in a stream?**

❯ **How do you hear the chirps and cheeps of birds?**

❯ **Why don't you fall off the planet?**

❯ **Why can't you touch a cloud?**

❯ **Why do puppies sleep piled on top of one other?**

All of these questions can be answered by science. After doing the experiments in this book, you'll be able to answer these questions and more. Although, once scientists can answer one question, they often come up with more questions. That's what's so great about science—it never ends!

The great scientist Albert Einstein once said, "No amount of experimentation can ever prove me right; a single experiment can prove me wrong." Some of these pages will have multiple projects to show the same point. With other projects, you'll be able to change and adapt the directions if you'd like to investigate a topic further. By doing similar experiments, you might reinforce a theory.

Great scientists are curious and want to do something with that curiosity. If you're constantly wanting to know how or why something happens, you could be a great scientist as well!

HOW THIS BOOK WORKS

Science in a Jar is divided into several chapters, each devoted to a different kind of science: life science, chemistry, earth science, physical science, and environmental science.

First, you may be asking, what is science? Simply put, it's observing, questioning, researching, and playing with ideas. Scientists are like artists who develop a system of asking and answering questions through a series of organized experiments. Sometimes these experiments go exactly as planned; other times, they may not. In the second case, scientists will ask more questions and do more experiments. It is also important for scientists to communicate their results so that others can learn from their work.

Each project in this book will provide you with a materials list, a procedure, and an observation section where we'll explore what happened. Some activities will offer extensions for further study. Others will explain how the science is being used today, and some will provide interesting and surprising facts.

Preparing Your Workspace

It's important to have a clean, dry workspace for many experiments. In some cases, you will work with water and food coloring, which may damage surfaces. Consider using a plastic tablecloth for anything that might stain or damage your table.

Supplies

Just about all of these projects use simple things you likely have in your home already. This is a great way to recycle materials you already have! All of the projects require a jar. Some projects can use a jar of any size, while others work best with a specific size. When a project does specify a size, it's usually because the measurements in the experiment are important. However, after you've completed each experiment, you'll soon figure out you can adapt it to suit your curiosity!

Throughout the book, you will see jars listed as small, medium, and large. Large jars hold 3 cups (720 ml), medium jars hold 1½ cups (360 ml), and small jars hold 1 cup (240 ml). Most jars you'll see in the photos are canning jars, like Mason jars. For a few projects you'll see Weck jars, which have a wider opening and can be easier to work with for some projects. The exceptions to this are the Elephant Toothpaste, which works best with a jar that has a narrow opening, and Artful Oceans, which calls for thinner jars found in a craft store.

THE SCIENTIFIC METHOD

Scientists follow a particular series of steps to stay organized and focused. This is called the scientific method. As you follow each project, refer back to this page and think like a scientist. What do you already know? What do you want to know? What can you do with the information you learn?

This cake has burnt edges, which is an indication that it was baked at too high of a temperature or for too long.

Step 1: Make observations

Scientists are constantly looking around, trying to figure out how things work or why they don't work. Say you're baking a cake and it turns out perfect! It's light and fluffy and tastes delicious. But the next time you use the same recipe, it turns out flat and a little burnt.

Step 2: Ask a question

These observations usually lead to a question, such as, "How come when I made this cake before it was so tasty, and now it looks and tastes like a burnt cracker?"

Step 3: Develop a hypothesis

A **hypothesis** is a possible answer to your question. If you do some research before your experiment and update your hypothesis, you will usually have a better chance of being right. In the cake example, you would review the ingredients of your cake. You recognize you might have left baking soda out of the batter the second time you made it.

Step 4:
Conduct an experiment

Finally! You get to test your idea with a super cool procedure. You'll want to write the procedure down so others can try it too. First, you'll bake a cake making sure you don't forget the baking soda. Then, you'll make a cake without any baking soda at all.

Step 5:
Form your conclusions

What did you learn from your experiment? Did leaving out the baking soda make a difference?

Step 6: Share your results

Don't be shy about teaching others what you learned! And it's okay if the activity doesn't work out quite right. That's just a part of science, and it's still worth sharing. Things rarely work out right the first time. It isn't a failure. You're learning what doesn't work! Be patient, have fun, and you might just learn something you didn't anticipate.

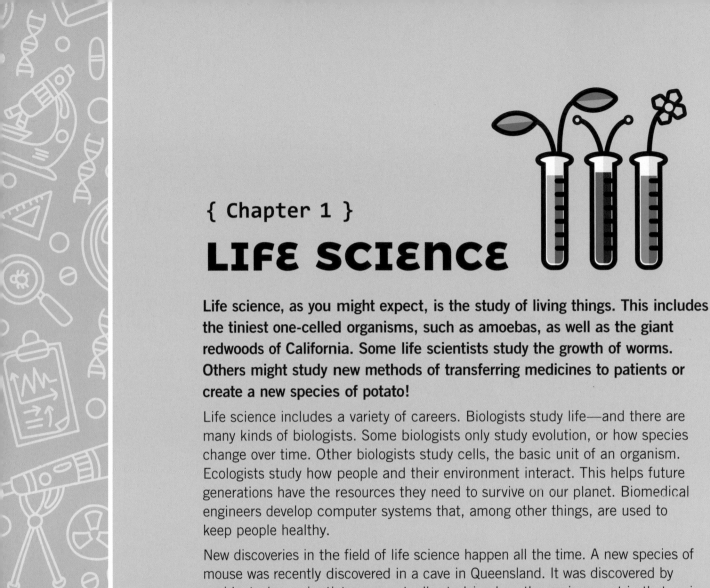

{ Chapter 1 }

LIFE SCIENCE

Life science, as you might expect, is the study of living things. This includes the tiniest one-celled organisms, such as amoebas, as well as the giant redwoods of California. Some life scientists study the growth of worms. Others might study new methods of transferring medicines to patients or create a new species of potato!

Life science includes a variety of careers. Biologists study life—and there are many kinds of biologists. Some biologists only study evolution, or how species change over time. Other biologists study cells, the basic unit of an organism. Ecologists study how people and their environment interact. This helps future generations have the resources they need to survive on our planet. Biomedical engineers develop computer systems that, among other things, are used to keep people healthy.

New discoveries in the field of life science happen all the time. A new species of mouse was recently discovered in a cave in Queensland. It was discovered by accident when scientists were actually studying how the environment in that region has changed over time. Researchers in Austin, Texas, have discovered chemicals in weed killers are likely killing the bee population. The chemical interferes with bacteria in the bees' guts. This is a critical problem for our food chain.

The projects on the following pages are an introduction to life science. As you do them, consider how scientists in the field might use them. How will they help you learn about the world we live in? What else can they teach you? After you do an experiment once, consider changing directions on your own to study new or different things.

EXPERIMENT #1

MATERIALS

- ❯ 1 small jar with lid
- ❯ Paper towels
- ❯ 3 beans (pinto, kidney, or any other dry bean)
- ❯ Water

Fee Fi Fo Fum!

GROW YOUR OWN BEANSTALK

How does a seed grow?

In this project, you can practice using the **scientific method** with a simple experiment.

Start by observing the plants and trees around you. Is your house or apartment full of beautiful plants on the windowsill? Or maybe a plant is brown and drooping in the corner all alone and depressed. If you happen to farm or garden, you'll probably notice some plants grow better than others.

But why? How come some plants grow better than others?

Create a hypothesis. Maybe your grandma has some plants in the sun and some in a darker room, such as the spare bedroom that only gets used when you visit her a couple of times a year. Perhaps she asks you to water them. This tells you plants need water to live. Your hypothesis might be, "Seeds need light and water to grow."

Scientists try to examine one idea at a time. This way they can learn one thing very well. For this

hold edgesexperiment, we'll focus on water. It's also important to gather all of the supplies you need to conduct your research.

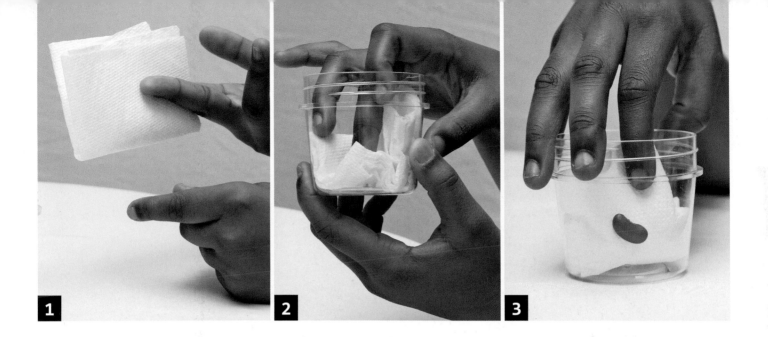

PROCEDURE

Now that you have all of the materials, it's time to get science-y! As you use this book, follow the procedure as you read it. Then, feel free to repeat the experiment. Try adding or changing a few steps to help you understand new things.

1 Fold a paper towel so it is the same height as the jar you are using.

2 Crumple more paper towels and place them in the middle of the jar. Use enough to keep the lined paper towel held against the outside of the jar.

3 Place three beans around the perimeter between the paper towel and the glass. The lined paper towel will hold them up. Be sure they are evenly spaced.

(CONTINUED)

→ **NOTE**

National Bean Day is January 6th, which is also a day to celebrate Gregor Mendel. Mendel famously used beans to test theories about how we inherit traits.

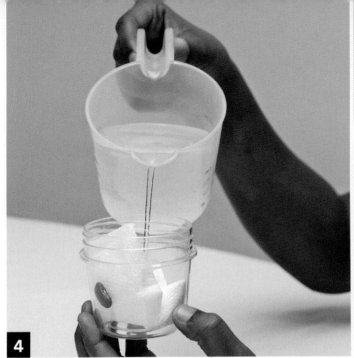

→ TRY THIS!

For a more involved experiment, you can determine how plants grow best by exploring these two options.

Option 1: In one jar, plant a bean just as you did here. That will be your **control**. Set up another jar the same way, but now fill it with water and keep the jar saturated. Set up a third jar as you did the first one, but keep it inside a cabinet where it won't get any light. Observe how the plants grow differently.

Option 2: Set up a control jar as directed above. Set up a second jar the same way, but place a lid on top. Which one sprouts faster?

4 Dampen the paper towels in the jar. They don't need to be soaked, just moist!

Hint: Your beans will sprout faster if you place the lid lightly on the jar rather than screwing it tightly in place.

5 Observe the beans as they begin to sprout.

6 It may take several days for germination, or growth of the seed, to begin. Make notes as you see the beans begin to change.

OBSERVATION

All of the things the plant needs to grow are packed inside those little beans. The bean is the seed of the plant. Once the seed gets the proper nutrients, such as water and sunlight, it germinates and grows into a mature plant. Plant food will also help the plant grow. With the help of food and water, that little bean will grow into a magical beanstalk.

This process is similar for most things, including people. The human body is made of 60 percent water. If you don't drink enough of the stuff, your cells won't thrive. Scientists say the human body can only last up to 1 week without water. And even though you can live a little longer without food, your body needs it to grow strong and healthy. Like the plant, your body converts food and water into the things it needs to survive.

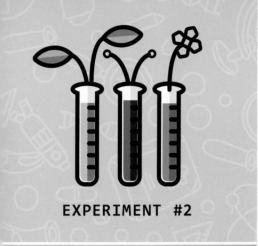

EXPERIMENT #2

CREATE A COLORFUL BOUQUET

How does a flower eat and drink?

In the first experiment, you watched how the beans started as hard, dry objects and turned into lush, green plants. You learned seeds need water. Seeds can't pick up a glass of ice-cold lemonade and take a sip. But they do use a straw, or something kind of like a straw. In this experiment, you'll see how plants "drink." At the end, you'll have colorful flowers to give to someone special!

MATERIALS

- ❯ 3 large jars
- ❯ Water
- ❯ Red, blue, and yellow food coloring
- ❯ 3 white carnations, chrysanthemums, or any other type of white flower

PROCEDURE

1 Fill each jar one-third with water.

2 Add a different color to each jar. You'll need approximately 5 drops. Use enough so that the water looks as tinted as the photos you see here. If you want to get creative, you can blend your food coloring choices—for example, use some yellow and some blue to make green.

3 Place a white flower in each jar and set it aside. It's best to put the flowers near a window or in a sunny spot.

(CONTINUED)

4

4 After the first day, look closely at the flowers. You should begin to see the color appearing on their petals.

5 After 3 to 5 days, the petals will be even more colorful. Look at the leaves. Do you see any change in color there?

OBSERVATION

Plants have roots, stems, and leaves. They need water to stay healthy. The water travels through the plant using capillary action. The flower pulls the water up through its stem. Chances are, the first thing you noticed was that the flowers changed color! But if you look very carefully, you will see the leaves changing color as well.

In a way, it's like the plant is sucking on a straw. Once the water has been pulled up through the plant, **transpiration** takes place. This is when the water leaves the plant and **evaporates** into the air. It's one reason the rainforest is so steamy! As the water evaporates into the atmosphere, the plant pulls up more water.

→ WHAT ABOUT A CACTUS?

Cactuses live in dry areas, but they still need water to live. They have lots of roots that work hard to soak up underground water. Their stems are designed to store this water for long periods of time. If you find yourself trapped in a desert but can get to a cactus, break it open. Chances are you can find lifesaving water inside!

MICROSCOPIC SWIMMERS

What's in pond water?

It may not seem like it, but our planet is mostly water. More than 70 percent of the Earth's surface is the blue stuff. That's a lot! Of that percentage, 96.5 percent of water is salt water. The rest is fresh water, which is less than 4 percent of all the water in our world. This is the water in lakes, in rivers, and in the air. Most fresh water is unavailable to humans. It's far beneath the Earth's surface. This groundwater keeps lakes and ponds from drying up and keeps rivers flowing.

Water is essential to the animals on our planet. Even a calm, quiet pond is teeming with life. Ponds are home to turtles, ducks, and various fish, but they are also home to much smaller creatures, such as amoebas and bacteria. All living things depend on one another for food. Even the tiny things you cannot see are important in the food chain.

In this project, you'll examine pond life to see some of the smallest critters in our ecosystem.

MATERIALS

- 1 large jar with lid
- Bucket
- Pond water (see steps 1 and 2)
- Magnifying lens

PROCEDURE

1 Locate the best place to access pond water. If you don't mind getting a little dirty, some of the muddier, squishier places have the best samples.

2 It's best to use the bucket to collect your water because it won't break if you accidentally drop it into the pond. Drag a bucket deep into the pond and pull out water. If you scoop out a bucket of pond water and it comes up clear, drag the bucket deeper under the surface. For a super exciting (yet gross) sample, drag the bucket along the bottom and get some of the squishy pond floor.

3 While the water in the bucket is still sloshing around, dip your jar into the bucket and collect a water sample. If you wait for the water to settle, you won't get as much pond life in your sample.

4 Screw the lid of the jar on tight and dump the rest of the water back in the pond.

Note: Some bacteria can make people sick. Coliform bacteria can cause waterborne illnesses. Ponds near farms can have larger amounts of animal waste, which can cause bad bacteria to build up. Make sure to wash your hands after collecting your sample.

5 When you get home, observe your water sample with the magnifying lens. If you have a hard time seeing the objects in the jar, place a white piece of paper on the opposite side of the jar. See anything? It might take some searching.

6 Let your pond water settle for a few hours. Once the plant matter has settled at the bottom, you'll still be able to see tiny organisms swimming around the jar.

OBSERVATION

Depending on where you collected your sample, you are likely to have a jar full of green plants of various sizes, and some teeny-tiny floating creatures. Green plants are known as **producers**. The food chain starts with these. They take energy from the sun and create their own food through a process called photosynthesis.

In some lakes, phytoplankton and algae are abundant. Algae are single-celled critters that don't have stems, roots, or leaves. They aren't even considered plants, but they do photosynthesize, or use sunlight to make their own food. Some algae, such as planktonic algae, makes water look hazy green, brown, or even red. This is often referred to as an algae bloom, which often consists of floating algae and is the beginning of the pond food chain.

Some of the tiniest animals in pond water are called rotifers. Rotifers mostly live in fresh water and have been found on every continent. They feed on bacteria. Slightly larger creatures feed on rotifers and algae. Because of this, teeny tiny critters such as algae and rotifers help transfer energy from the sun to animals higher up the food chain.

→ TRY THIS!

To take this experiment to another level, take another sample. Go to a river and use the bucket to collect water. Then, like before, scoop a glass jar into the bucket to get your sample. Label each jar according to where you collected the water. Then, make notes about the types and numbers of organisms you see.

The more variety the better. Try different ponds, or different places in the same pond. Visit rivers of different sizes, or even the ocean. Ponds won't always have the diversity that rivers do. This is because oftentimes ponds are seasonal, and they are isolated. This means not as many critters will enter the water. In a large river, however, more species find their way to the water sources, so many different organisms will be found there.

SLITHERY SOIL DWELLERS

What do earthworms do for the environment?

Have you ever wandered outside after a storm and noticed all the worms? Where do they come from? And what's the point of a worm? What does it do? They may not be cute and cuddly, but earthworms are critical in maintaining our planet. Ecologists even call earthworms a keystone species because of their importance. Before we get into all the gritty details, let's get to the experiment. You can make an earthworm habitat and study these crucial creatures for a few weeks. Just be sure to let them go when you're done!

MATERIALS

- 1 large jar
- 1 small can or small jar (a soup can will work)
- Sand
- Damp (but not wet) soil
- 6 to 8 worms
- Compost or mulched leaves
- Cloth or aluminum foil
- Rubber band
- Dark construction paper
- Tape
- Pin

PROCEDURE

1 Place the can or small jar on the bottom of the large jar, upside down. Once you fill the large jar, this will keep the worms pushed out to the sides of the jar so you can see them.

2 Add a layer of sand to the bottom of the jar, about ½ inch (1 cm) deep.

3 Add a layer of soil on top of the sand layer, about 1 inch (2.5 cm) deep.

4 Alternate the layers of sand and soil until the jar is nearly full. The top layer must be soil!

5 Place the worms on top of the soil.

6 Cover the worms with the leaves or compost.

7 Cover the jar lid with the cloth or foil and secure it with the rubber band. Use the pin to poke airholes in the top.

8   Observe the worms for a little bit, then cover the sides of the jar with the construction paper and secure with tape. There's a reason you don't see worms tanning themselves! They like the dark.

9   Place the jar in a dark, cool place.

10 Check on the worms each day. Watch how they burrow. Just be sure to cover the jar with the paper when you aren't observing.

11 Care for the worms while you are observing them. Make sure the soil stays moist. You can use an eyedropper to add water to the jar, or simply let water drip from your fingers into the habitat. Once a week, feed the worms. Small pieces of ripe fruit or vegetables will work. You can also add more leaves or compost.

12 After about a month, you should return the worms to the earth.

→ FUN FACT

Worms poop 1.5 times their body weight each day! Could you imagine if people did that?

OBSERVATION

Earthworms break down organic matter and fertilize the soil. They'll eat leaves and small organisms on top of the soil. You may not notice them eating, but you will see the top layer in the jar change as they do their work. If worms are underground, they'll munch on bacteria and fungi. All of this helps the planet because their poop (also called castings) is full of bacteria and nutrients that plants need to grow. In studies, soil in areas rich with worms had five times the nutrients of non-worm locations.

Worms also help **aerate** the soil. Notice how they loosen and mix up soil as they burrow and tunnel around. Then more plants can grow deeper roots. It also helps because the nutrients have been mixed around in the dirt. All of this tunneling helps prevent **erosion** and flooding because water can fill up the holes made by worms.

So, if you see a worm needing help crossing the street as the sun dries the pavement, consider helping that worm to a nice, moist spot. They are incredibly important animals!

→ NOTE

This experiment requires a large jar so that the worms can grow. In this experiment, we used a jar that held 5 cups (1,200 ml). Time for a disclaimer, though—the first worms we caught were pretty thin, and they were hard to see. If you have skinny worms, you'll want a 3-cup (720 ml) jar. If you get nice, fat worms, you'll want the bigger jar.

HUDDLE FOR HEAT

Why do animals snuggle when they sleep?

On a cold winter morning, it's hard to get out of bed! Snuggling under the blankets is far more appealing. But what if you don't have a pile of blankets to enjoy? What if you're a puppy? Or a little baby mouse? What's a puppy to do? Pile up, of course! In the science world, this cute little practice can be referred to as huddling.

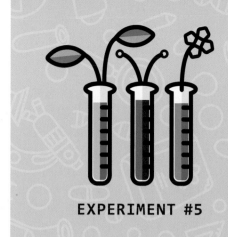

EXPERIMENT #5

MATERIALS

> 7 small jars

Note: You'll need enough jars to have one jar alone, and the rest will make a circle with one jar in the middle. They must all be able to touch.

> Water

> Dual-probe thermometer (or you can use 2 thermometers)

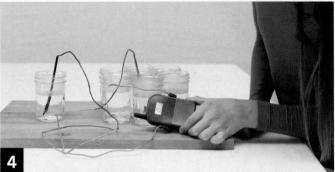

PROCEDURE

----

1 Organize the jars. One jar will stand lonely off to the side of the others, representing a lonely puppy. The rest will be connected. Set one jar on the table and place all other jars around it, making sure they are all touching. The jar by itself and the jar in the middle of the huddle are the test jars.

2 Heat the water. You can simply use hot water from the tap, or use the stove or microwave to heat the water. Just make sure to stir the water so the temperature is even throughout the container. Our starting temperature was 115°F (46°C).

3 Pour an equal amount of water in each of the jars that represent the "huddle." Finally, pour water into each test jar—the jar in the middle of the pack and the jar off to the side. You may want to say nice things to the lonely jar so it doesn't feel so bad!

4 If you are using a dual-probe thermometer, place a probe in each test jar. If you are using two thermometers, place one in each test jar. Just be sure to make note of the temperature of each thermometer. This way you will have accurate results.

5 Record the temperature of each test jar immediately. Then, every minute for 5 minutes, observe and record the temperature.

OBSERVATION

You should notice the lonely jar is cooling off faster than the test jar in the middle of the heap. While at first it may only seem like a few degrees' difference, imagine being that little animal on the outside cooling off first!

→ HOW ANIMALS USE THIS SCIENCE

Energy is the constant flow of heat, and heat is continuously flowing in and out of objects. As you just saw, heat flows from hot to cold.

This is why puppies snuggle together. If they are surrounded by the same temperature, the heat doesn't flow away from their bodies. This keeps them warmer longer. Meerkats do this as well. Often, the leaders of the pack stay in the middle of the fuzzy lump. The heat won't leave their bodies as quickly. It might not be fun to be the little fella on the outside—they'll cool off first.

Nowadays, many people have indoor heat and heavy coats to stay warm. But that wasn't always the case. People in cold climates often slept huddled with their animals. And there are diaries explaining how people in the 1800s would pack together in beds to stay warm, just like many animals do.

{ Chapter 2 }

CHEMISTRY

Chemistry is the study of matter and its properties. Every material in the world is made up of matter. Matter takes up space and has something called mass. Your favorite food is matter. Your guts are matter. Your stinky socks hidden under your bed are matter.

Matter takes on different properties. Water is an easy example. You drink it, you ice skate on it, and you see it as steam when you make mac and cheese. This is chemistry.

Chemists study how mixing substances can change properties. When you mix substances and properties, a new substance can be created. Without the water, spaghetti wouldn't be much fun to eat. But boil those noodles in water and you've got some yummy pasta. This is chemistry.

There are many types of chemistry. Organic chemistry has to do with the chemistry of living things. Biochemistry studies the chemical processes in living things. For example, how do cells break down and use sugar?

Inorganic chemistry studies chemical reactions between nonliving things, like metals and minerals. Some types of gasoline are used for rockets, but you wouldn't use the same gas in your lawnmower. This is also chemistry!

The following experiments examine different kinds of chemistry. As you explore, notice how elements interact (or don't interact) with each other.

MIX IT UP

Why don't oil and water mix?

If you've ever had to shake a bottle of salad dressing before pouring it, this project will look familiar! The fancy words to describe this are *hydrophobic interaction*. Put more simply, that's when two substances, such as oil and water, only stay mixed for a short time before separating again. Let's investigate why.

MATERIALS

- ❯ 1 small jar with lid
- ❯ Water
- ❯ Cooking oil (olive oil, vegetable oil, any oil you have at home)

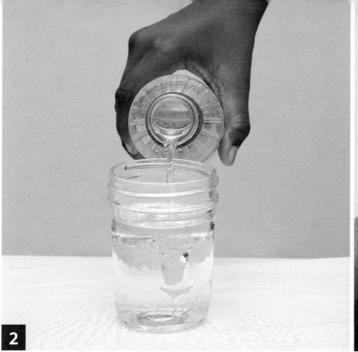

PROCEDURE

1 Fill the jar a little more than half full with water.

2 Add the oil, 1 tablespoon (15 ml) at a time. Use the photo as a guide or add more. It's up to you how much you'd like to add.

3 Check it out! What does it look like?

4 Secure the lid and shake that jar fast.

5 Observe the oil and water mixture. What's happening?

OBSERVATION

Do the oil and water mix? It might look like they do at first, but look closer. Molecule in the oil are attracted to other oil molecules and therefore exclude the water. You'll also notice the oil rests on top of the water. This is because water is denser than oil. Molecules in water are more compact, causing them to tighten together. This makes a stronger base for the oil to float on.

{ Experiment #6 Variation }
WHAT DOES DISH SOAP DO?

OBSERVATION

The clear line between oil and water vanished. Now it's one happy jar of liquid. What gives? Dish soap is the bridge to unifying both oil and water. One end of the soap molecule attaches to the water molecules. The other end of the soap molecule attaches to the oil. Once the oil and water are linked, the grease will be removed from the object. Then it can be wiped away and you have a clean plate!

Let's try something new! Have you seen soap commercials that claim a product is tough on dirt and grease? How does that work? Time to find out.

PROCEDURE

1 Pour some dish soap into your oil/water mixture.

2 Give it a shake.

3 Observe as the new solution settles. This might take a while if it got good and bubbly!

ELEPHANT TOOTHPASTE

What causes chemical reactions?

Let's create some explosions! First, warm up with the small reaction on page 42. Then come back here and let's make something really foamy. This is a similar process to the baking soda reaction but will have a more explosive result! If you'd like to turn this into a longer experiment, try changing the variables a bit. What happens if you add more yeast? Or more dish soap? You can also change the width and height of the bottle to see how that changes your results.

EXPERIMENT #7

MATERIALS

- 1 large jar
- 1 mixing bowl
- 3 tablespoons (45 ml) of warm water
- 1 tablespoon (12 g) or single packet of active, dry yeast
- Pan or baking sheet to contain the mess you are about to create!
- 1 small mixing spoon
- ½ cup (120 ml) 3% to 6% hydrogen peroxide (found in drugstores)
- Food coloring
- Liquid dish soap

1

3

4

PROCEDURE

----

1 Mix the warm water and the yeast in the mixing bowl. Stir well, then set off to the side.

2 Place the jar in the pan. Nothing exciting to see here, it's just going to make your clean up easier!

3 Pour the hydrogen peroxide into the jar.

4 Add 5 drops of color and mix it a bit.

Tip: You can be creative here. If you want striped toothpaste, drip colors down the side of the jar. You can also drop a few different colors, but don't mix it. Just see what happens!

5 Add a squirt of dish soap and swirl the jar around a few times.

6 Now add the yeast mixture to the hydrogen peroxide and watch the reaction! If you don't mind getting a little sticky, touch the side of the jar. Does it feel warm? It should!

OBSERVATION

Hydrogen peroxide is an unstable substance. It breaks down easily, and when it does, oxygen is released. If you've ever used hydrogen peroxide on a cut, you'll notice it fizzes a little bit. The higher the percentage of hydrogen peroxide, the more fizz. But you also wouldn't want to pour higher concentrations of hydrogen peroxide on your skin!

The yeast contains an enzyme called catalase. Catalase can be found in most plants and animals, including people. The catalase (in this case, yeast) sped up the chemical reaction without changing the product. In this experiment, the yeast sped up the process of breaking down the hydrogen peroxide into oxygen and water. Then, the oxygen got trapped in the soap, producing the foam. This chemical reaction is called an exothermic reaction. This is because the energy created during the experiment is released as heat.

→ **NOTE**

For this project, it's best to find a jar that holds at least 5 cups (1,200 ml), and one that has an opening that is narrower than the body (such as a standard-size, rather than widemouthed, Mason jar).

BAKING SODA EXPLOSION

MATERIALS

- 3 tablespoons (41 g) baking soda
- Vinegar
- Mixing bowl

OBSERVATION

Baking soda and vinegar react with each other because they exchange **atoms**. Baking soda is a **base**, and it wants a **proton**. The vinegar is an acid, and it will get rid of a proton. When the acid gives the base a proton, it creates the exciting fizzing result you just saw!

A science project book wouldn't be a science project book without baking soda explosions! Do you know why baking soda is used for baking? Baking soda, also called sodium bicarbonate, is a natural chemical **compound**. When it is mixed with an **acid** (in this case, vinegar), it creates carbon dioxide. This makes the bubbles you'll see in this experiment. In baking, it gives cakes and cookies a fluffy texture. In science experiments, it creates a super fun mess. So beware: The experiment you're about to do will definitely create an explosive (yet safe!) result.

PROCEDURE

1 Place the baking soda in the jar.

2 Pour vinegar over the baking soda until it starts to have a reaction. You'll know it's happening because you'll see bubbles.

3 Stand back!

STINKY SOLUTIONS

What are acids and bases?

Chemists work with solutions known as acids and bases. These acids and bases are a part of our everyday life. Acids in our stomach kill bacteria to keep us healthy. Our pancreas produces a base that helps us digest food. The orange juice you drank for breakfast is acidic, but the toothpaste you used afterward is a base.

Almost all objects are either acids or bases. You can do this simple project to see if items in your kitchen are an acid or a base.

EXPERIMENT #8

MATERIALS

- 1 red cabbage
- Blender
- 2 cups (480 ml) water
- Colander
- 4 glass jars
- Vinegar
- Mixing spoons
- 2 tablespoons (28 g) baking soda
- 1 lemon

PROCEDURE

----

1 Pull about five to six cabbage leaves from the cabbage and place them in the blender. Process for 1 minute at high speed. The cabbage will be well shredded.

2 Add the water.

3 Place the colander over one of the glass jars.

4 Carefully pour the cabbage juice through the colander, which will collect the meatier parts of the cabbage you don't need. Keep the jar of purple cabbage juice.

5 Carefully pour ½ cup (120 ml) of the cabbage juice into each of the remaining three jars.

6 Add 2 tablespoons (30 ml) of vinegar to the first jar and mix well.

7 Add the baking soda to the second jar and mix well with the second spoon. Don't reuse the same spoon!

8 Squeeze a portion of the lemon into the third jar and mix it well with the third spoon. How did the jars of cabbage juice change?

5

8

In this project, the cabbage acts as an indicator. When an acid or base is mixed with an indicator, the indicator will change colors to reveal whether the liquid is an acid or a base. Acidic solutions will appear red while base solutions will turn the indicator greenish.

Acids and bases can be measured on the pH scale. Any substance measuring 1 to 6 on this scale is an acid. A substance measuring 8 to 14 on the scale is a base. If a substance scores a 7 on the scale, it is called neutral. Water has a pH of 7.

Test other items around your house to see whether each is an acid or a base. You can even drop in various foods. Try things such as rubbing alcohol, sugar, or various juices.

→ CROSS-CONTAMINATION

Scientists must be careful of something called cross-contamination. This means when you stir each solution, you must use a clean spoon. Otherwise, your experiment may not teach you what you are hoping to learn. For example, some of the acid from the vinegar may mix into the solution with baking soda. This would interfere with the experiment and not give a correct result.

BOUNCING EGGS

How can vinegar transform a fragile egg into a bouncing ball?

An egg, as we know it, is very fragile. The gentlest tap can cause it to crack and break. But is there a way to make it bounce? Seeing as this experiment is called Bouncing Eggs, the answer is yes! Careful, though—bouncing your egg may take a few attempts.

MATERIALS

> ❷ 2 medium glass jars with lids

> ❷ 1 cup (240 ml) vinegar

> ❷ 2 raw eggs, plus a few extras in case they break

> ❷ 1 spoon large enough to hold an egg

> ❷ 1 cup (240 ml) corn syrup

> ❷ Water

PROCEDURE

1 Fill the two jars with vinegar.

2 Place an egg in each jar. Use a spoon to help you carefully lower the egg into the jar so it doesn't crack.

3 Pour vinegar over each egg. Secure the lid tightly. What do you see? These bubbles are carbon dioxide gas. It proves the reaction is working.

4 Observe what happens to the eggs over the next 24 hours. On day 2, you'll see the egg's shell has dissolved.

5 Very gently, pour out the vinegar. Use the spoon to gently remove the egg from the jar.

6 Very carefully, rinse the egg in warm water. If any shell is left, it will rub off in your hands. Just be careful not to puncture the egg's membrane.

7 Hold the egg 3 inches (7.5 cm) above a table and gently drop (don't throw!) the egg. Does it bounce?

(CONTINUED)

OBSERVATION

The shell has dissolved because of the acetic acid in the vinegar, but the membrane surrounding the egg has not. It will be soft and squishy to the touch. You can even bounce the egg, but bounce it gently. It is still fragile. Another cool thing is to darken the room and get a flashlight. Place the flashlight behind the egg and take a look. Can you see the yolk inside?

PROCEDURE (CONTINUED)

8   Now clean the jars. Fill one with corn syrup and the other with water.

9   Gently place a naked egg in each jar.

10   Observe the egg in each jar. Which one floats? Which one sinks?

11   Leave the eggs in the jars for 24 hours, then remove them. How do they look? Which one is bigger?

→ **NOTE**

In some cases, the eggshell might peel off but stay in one big piece. Consider yourself lucky! It will be soft and moveable. You can create some egg-cellent artwork. Just shape it and let it dry.

OBSERVATION

The egg that was in the corn syrup should be smaller. This is because the corn syrup has sugar molecules. They are too large to pass through the egg membrane. On the other hand, water molecules can pass through the membrane. The water molecules moved from the jar into the egg, expanding the size of the egg.

If you'd like to do a fun (but messy) experiment, bounce the egg from 1 inch (2.5 cm) off a surface. Does it break? Probably not, as long as you dropped it gently. Then drop it from 2 inches (5 cm) above a surface. Does it break? At what point does it finally break?

→ TRY THIS!

Try this experiment with other liquids. What else will dissolve the shell? Try soda, orange juice, rubbing alcohol, or lemon juice. If you are nervous to try it with a raw egg, try using a hard-boiled egg instead. For a colorful experiment, color the vinegar solution with food coloring.

MATERIALS

- ❯ 1 large jar (with lid for storage)
- ❯ About 1 cup (240 ml) of glue
- ❯ About ¼ cup (60 ml) of liquid laundry detergent
- ❯ Mixing spoon

THE SLIME WORKSHOP

How does slime work?

The slime craze is certainly a fun one, but it's also very scientific. Have you wondered why some slime is stickier than other kinds, or why some seems fluffier? And what makes the slime stick to itself anyhow? The answers include super fancy words such as **monomer** and **polymer**.

Many liquids are made of unconnected molecules moving around. These are single molecules that don't stick together. One example is water. On the other hand, there are substances that are made of many monomers stuck, or bonded, together. These are called polymers. These chains of monomers can be long, and you can pull these chains apart.

When you add a substance that makes the bonds stick together, they won't come apart anymore. All of these polymers will stay together, but still be flexible and gooey. And sticky. Or fluffy. Or noisy! So what does this have to do with slime? Let's make a batch of slime first, and then break down how the science works. When you understand the science, you can develop your own custom slime recipe!

PROCEDURE

You don't need precise measurements when you make slime. That's part of the fun!

1 Pour some glue into the jar. Try 1 cup (240 ml) to start with, though you can also try different amounts and get different results. The amount of glue you use will change how the slime feels.

2 Mix in the detergent, just a little bit at a time. The standard ratio for slime is four parts glue to one part detergent. This means if you used 1 cup (240 ml) of glue, add ¼ cup (60 ml) of detergent. But it's up to you! How sticky do you like your slime?

3 Remove the slime from the jar and enjoy.

OBSERVATION

The glue acted as a polymer. A polymer is like a paper chain. It has a molecular structure that is bonded together. The polymer in the glue moves easily from the bottle to your jar. Its molecules don't stick together, but they will stick to other objects.

When you added the detergent, the bonds in the detergent caused the glue molecules to stick together, creating a slime. They are still flexible and can move, but not as easily.

CUSTOMIZE YOUR SLIME

This is where you can really have fun in your laboratory. Now that you have a basic slime recipe, explore a variety of ingredients. Here are some ideas to add to the slime you made on the previous page with about 1 cup (240 ml) of glue and ¼ cup (60 ml) of detergent.

Once you are done playing with your slime, keep it in your jar with the lid closed tight. It will last for weeks, unless you've added vinegar (see below).

BAKING SODA

This base will bubble a bit as you add it to the mixture. Add 1 tablespoon (14 g) at a time. You'll see how the slime gets fluffier. In fact, another popular slime recipe is glue, baking soda, and a bit of saline solution. In this recipe, the saline solution acts like the detergent, bonding the glue together.

INSTANT SNOW

Using instant snow in your slime is nothing less than awesome! Just making a batch of instant snow is beyond cool. There are two ways to use instant snow powder in your slime. You can mix a batch of snow first by mixing the powder with water (and don't take your eyes off the snow when you add the water—it will POOF!) so you can play with it before adding it to your slime. Or, you can add 1 tablespoon (15 g) of the powder to the slime and then add 1 teaspoon (5 ml) of water and watch it POOF within the slime. Either way, it'll POOF and be super cool. If at first the instant snow doesn't seem to make a difference, just wait. As the powder absorbs more liquid, little beads will begin to swell. The more they swell, the stickier it will get. It may take 10 minutes before you see the best results.

VINEGAR

Add 1 tablespoon (15 ml) at a time and watch your slime slowly dissolve!

Note: You may want to save experimenting with vinegar until the end. It's likely you won't be able to play with your slime anymore once you've added this acid.

  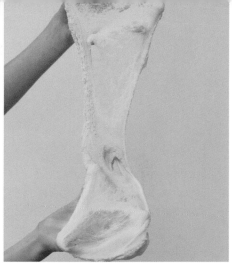

FOOD COLORING AND GLITTER

Adding food coloring and glitter to your slime will make it pretty! Just don't add too much at once or you'll have a mess on your hands. It's best to use one drop of food coloring at a time. When it comes to glitter, a dash here or a pinch there should be plenty to get you started. Of course, scientists are pretty cool with messes. Your parents, on the other hand, might not be.

→ LET'S GET NON-NEWTONIAN

Isaac Newton was a scientist that lived in the late 1600s to early 1700s. He observed that some fluid is affected by temperature. If ketchup is cold, it takes forever to drip out of the bottle. When it's warmer, it oozes faster. Slime, however, is considered a non-Newtonian fluid. Non-Newtonian fluids are affected by things other than temperature. Squeezing, pulling, and stretching are examples. When you stretch your slime slowly, it may pull apart and be ooey-gooey. But pull it fast and it will rip cleanly apart. See? It's a non-Newtonian fluid!

{ Chapter 3 }

EARTH SCIENCE

Earth science is actually out of this world! But what does that mean, exactly? It means earth science includes not only the study of the Earth, but also the study of space and other planets. There are four basic areas of earth science:

- **Geology**, which is the physical structures on a planet. Geologists study organisms of the planet and how the planet has changed over time. Geologists also study minerals, natural hazards, and ways to protect the planet in the future.

- **Meteorology**, which is the study of the atmosphere. Meteorologists work to learn how weather patterns are changing. They hope to better predict natural disasters in order to keep people safe.

- **Oceanography**, which is the study of the physical and biological components of the Earth's oceans. The oceans impact weather patterns. They are also changing as the atmosphere of the planet is changing.

- **Astronomy**, which is the study of the universe. Some astronomers study how the sun impacts the Earth's weather and climate. Astronomers also study landforms on other planets in an effort to understand our planet better.

The following projects will explore these four areas. As you do them, consider how earth scientists use the information to help understand our planet.

WHIRLING, TWIRLING TWISTERS

How do tornadoes form, and why are they dangerous?

Weather fanatics love a good tornado! Not because of the destruction they cause—they can cause a lot of damage. Tornadoes are incredible examples of how strong nature is. Tornadoes happen when warm, moist air is lifted by cooler air. When warm air and cool air meet, the atmosphere becomes unstable because the two weather patterns collide.

Winds often blow at different speeds. A simple change in wind direction and an increase in wind speed can create a horizontal spinning effect in the lower atmosphere. The warmer air will begin to rise, changing the wind from spinning horizontally to vertically. If the spinning column of air touches the ground, it is called a tornado. Otherwise, the proper name is a funnel cloud.

Making a safe tornado is easy to do. Then you can watch the awesome shape of a tornado from the safety of your kitchen!

MATERIALS

- 1 large jar with lid
- Water
- ½ tablespoon (8 ml) vinegar
- ½ tablespoon (8 ml) dish soap
- ½ teaspoon glitter, or small plastic trinkets to act as debris

PROCEDURE

1 Fill the jar with water until it's about two-thirds full.

2 Add the vinegar, then add the dish soap.

3 Swirl the jar in a twisting motion. You will see a tornado appear.

4 Now let's add a few objects of different masses to see how they are impacted by the tornado. Add some glitter or plastic objects of different sizes to your tornado. When you swirl the jar, what happens?

→ **TIP:**

If you've shaken the jar too much, the dish soap may make the water a bit bubbly. Let the suds settle and twirl the jar again.

OBSERVATION

A tornado is a rotating column of air, but in this case, you made a rotating column of water! The **vortex** of the tornado is the spinning column that you created. When you poured in the glitter (and other plastic objects you may have used), notice how it was swept along with the current. This is because the powerful twisting action lifts and pulls objects (debris) along with it. Think of objects a tornado might encounter. Flying bricks and wood from buildings could become very dangerous!

→ MEASURING TORNADOES

Tornadoes aren't measured by their height or weight like you are. Tornadoes are measured on the Fujita scale, or F scale. In the United States, the scale was updated in 2007 to account for property damage. This scale is called the EF scale. An EF-0 tornado is the lowest score, but winds will still be measured at 85 miles per hour (137 km/h). This tornado causes light damage. The most damaging tornadoes are labeled as EF-5 tornadoes. Winds measure over 200 miles per hour (322 km/h). These tornadoes have been known to kill hundreds of people and flatten homes and businesses. Aren't you glad your tornado is in a jar?

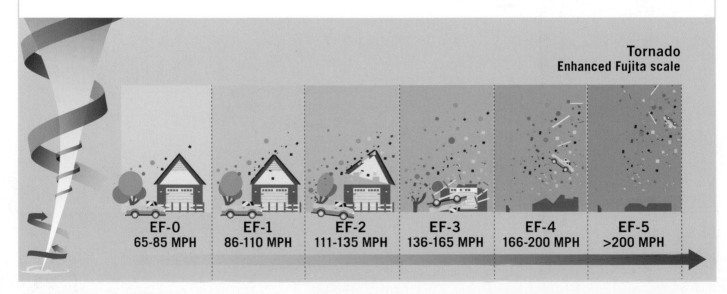

Tornado
Enhanced Fujita scale

| EF-0 | EF-1 | EF-2 | EF-3 | EF-4 | EF-5 |
| 65-85 MPH | 86-110 MPH | 111-135 MPH | 136-165 MPH | 166-200 MPH | >200 MPH |

ARTFUL OCEANS

What does it look like under the sea?

Scientists believe between 700,000 and 1,000,000 different species lives in the ocean. Many of them haven't been discovered or named yet! Scientists do know that there are five different layers of the ocean. This experiment will show you why different animals live in different parts of the ocean.

EXPERIMENT #12

MATERIALS

- 5 small, narrow jars (see photo above)
- Water
- Blue food coloring
- Flashlight
- 1 piece of white printer paper

PROCEDURE

----

1 Pour the same amount of water into each jar.

2 In Jar 1, squeeze one drop of blue food coloring. In Jar 2, squeeze two drops. Guess how many you'll put in Jar 3? It's three drops! Put four drops in Jar 4 and five drops in Jar 5.

3 Line up the jars in order. Observe the differences between the jars.

4 Place the jars, in order, against a sunny window. What do you notice?

5 Now move the jars to a darkened room. Hold a white piece of paper in front of the jars.

6 Shine a light from behind the jars onto the paper. Which jar allows the most light to pass? The least?

7 Leave the jars in a sunny space. Take and record the temperature of each jar. Is there a difference in temperature? In the ocean, the deeper water stays cooler due to the lack of sunlight. How do you think the temperature difference impacts animals that live in the ocean?

OBSERVATION

When you lined the jars up lightest to darkest, you made a model of the ocean's layers. The first jar was the lightest shade of blue and represents the surface level of the ocean. The fifth jar was the darkest shade of blue and represents the deepest levels. When you used the flashlight to see how much light passed through each jar, the flashlight represented the sun, and the jars showed you how light passes through each layer of the ocean.

The deepest part of the ocean is the hadalpelagic zone, also referred to as the trenches. This zone doesn't stretch across every ocean because it only exists where there are the deepest trenches. No plants live here because no light can reach these depths. Very few species can exist this far below the surface. Those that do feed on debris that has sunk to the bottom of the ocean. Above the hadapelagic zone is the abyssopelagic zone. Natural light does not reach these zones. The pressure of these lowest layers is high because of the weight of the water above them.

The middle layer is the bathypelagic zone. Species here are either black or red. This is because of the low sunlight penetration.

With such little blue-green light reflected from above, red actually appears black in this zone. It provides a perfect defense against predators.

The second-deepest layer is the mesopelagic zone. Many of the animals here use bioluminescence. This means the fish have a chemical that acts almost as a flashlight. When the sun isn't bright in the sky, the fish can use bioluminescence to see.

The top layer is the epipelagic zone. Here, the water is warmest and is home to coral reefs. This zone has enough light for plants to survive. For this reason, it's the only zone where plants can grow.

BALLOON MAGIC

What is air pressure?

Air pressure is the weight of air molecules pressing down on Earth. You typically don't feel the pressure, but it does exist. The greatest air pressure is at sea level. As you move higher into the atmosphere, the air pressure is lower. There are two ways air pressure can be increased or decreased. Adding molecules to an area will increase the air pressure, such as when you inflate your bike tire. A second way is with the increase or decrease of heat. That's what we'll see in this experiment.

EXPERIMENT #13

MATERIALS

- 1 large jar
- 1 balloon
- Water
- Paper
- Long-handled lighter

1

3

4

PROCEDURE

1 Fill the balloon with water. You'll want it big enough to sit on top of the jar comfortably. For best results, squish the balloon around to make it a bit more stretchy.

2 Place the balloon on top of the jar and observe it. Does it fall through the opening? It shouldn't! If it does, add more water. Now place the balloon off to the side.

3 With help from an adult, light the paper on fire and place it inside the jar.

4 Quickly place the water balloon on top of the jar and watch what happens!

OBSERVATION

When you first set the balloon on the jar in step 2, the air pressure in the jar was the same as the air pressure outside the jar. Nothing happened, and you probably thought this experiment was pretty boring. But when you placed the burning paper inside the jar, it caused the air inside the jar to heat and expand. If your balloon started dancing a little jig, this is because the expanding air was escaping around the sides of the balloon. Once the fire consumed all of the oxygen inside the jar, it went out. That's because fire needs oxygen. When the oxygen was gone, so was the fire. Then the air inside the jar cooled down. This cooler air takes up less space inside the jar. The air pressure on the outside of the balloon was greater than the air pushing up from the jar. And presto! The balloon slithered into the jar.

→ TRY THIS!

Repeat this experiment a few times. Sometimes, the balloon appears to get sucked into the jar slowly. Other times, it moves a bit faster. Why do you think this is?

As you repeat the experiment, you probably want to take your balloon out of the jar. If you pull on the balloon to take it out, it may be pretty stuck! A simple trick is to insert a straw along the side of the balloon and jar, allowing air pressure to get back into the jar. That will make it easier to get the balloon out.

SALTWATER FLASHLIGHTS

How do you build a conductivity meter?

Conductors are materials that allow electricity to pass through. Not all things are conductors, and we wouldn't want them to be. Otherwise we'd be getting electrocuted every day! Conductors are usually metals, but not always. Water by itself is not a conductor, but it can be with the right addition. In this project, you'll build a flashlight and then use it to determine what kinds of materials act as conductors. The results just might surprise you!

MATERIALS

- 3 medium jars
- 1 string of non-LED Christmas lights
- Wire strippers
- Wire cutters
- Aluminum foil
- 1 9-volt battery
- Tape
- 1 craft stick
- Water
- Salt
- Baking soda

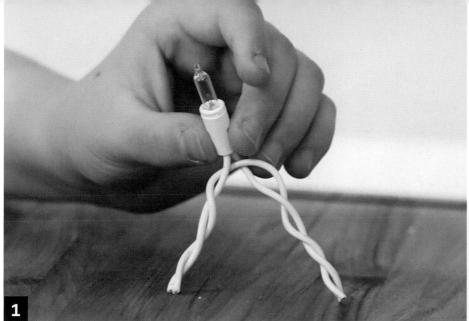

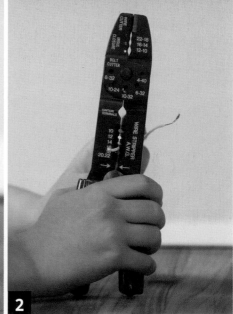

PROCEDURE

1 Make sure your lights are unplugged, then cut a light from the Christmas lights, making sure the two wires stay connected. They should be about 2 inches (5 cm) long.

2 Using wire strippers, strip the plastic coating to expose less than ½ inch (1 cm) of wiring.

3 Wrap a piece of aluminum foil around one of the exposed wires of the bulb.

4 Push the foil-wrapped wire into the positive terminal of the battery. Use tape to secure it in place.

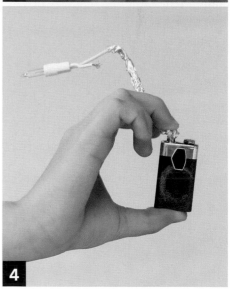

(CONTINUED)

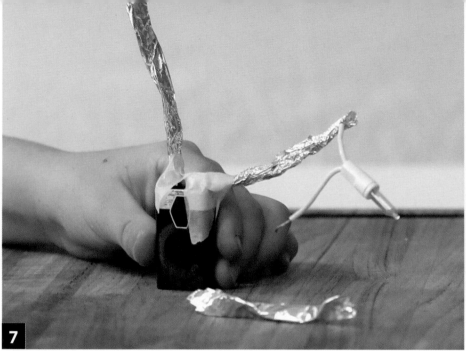

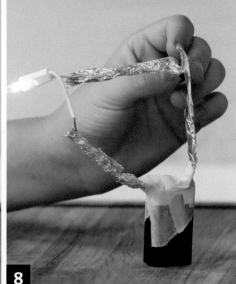

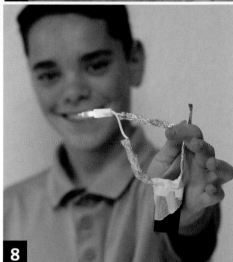

5 Roll two pieces of aluminum foil into two tubes. These will be the leads that test the conductivity of your test solutions.

6 Push the end of one of the aluminum leads into the negative terminal of the battery, then secure it with tape.

7 Wrap the other aluminum foil lead around the second exposed wire of the light.

8 Test the circuit by touching the two pieces of aluminum foil together. If the light glows, the circuit is complete. You are ready to move on with the experiment. However, if the light does not glow, there is a breakdown in the circuit. Double-check that the aluminum foil is connected to the 9-volt battery. The leads may have come loose in all of the scientific excitement!

WHAT'S A CIRCUIT?
WHAT ARE CONDUCTORS?

An electric circuit is simply a path that an **electric current** can pass through. If the circuit is open, the electricity cannot flow completely. However, when you close a circuit, electricity can flow. Circuits include a cell (in this case, the battery), the load or resistor (the light bulb), the switch (the aluminum foil leads), and a conductor (the wires).

1 Assemble your conductor. Tape the battery to the flat end of a craft stick. Make sure the aluminum leads hang down under the craft stick.

2 Fill your three jars with water. Add nothing to the first jar. In the second, add 1 tablespoon (18 g) of salt. In the third jar, add 1 tablespoon (14 g) of baking soda. Mix them well.

3 Place your conductor over the jar of water. Make sure the aluminum wires don't touch! What happens?

4 Now place the conductor over the jar of salt water. What happens now? Again, make sure the wires don't touch.

5 Finally, place the conductor over the jar of soda water. What happens this time?

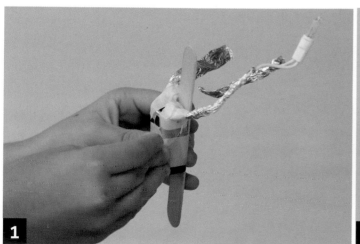

OBSERVATION

If the light bulb lit up in the solution, then the liquid is conductive. This means it contains electrolytes. Electrolytes are charged particles. They may be positively or negatively charged. Positive charges are attracted to negative charges, and negative charges are attracted to positive charges. This is where that phrase "opposites attract" comes from. In this experiment, the positively charged particles were attracted to the negative aluminum lead (remember the positive and negative terminals of the battery?), and as you can probably guess, the negative particles were attracted to the positive aluminum lead. The flow of these particles formed a complete circuit, allowing the light bulb to glow!

→ TRY THIS!

The fun doesn't have to stop here! You can test all kinds of things for conductivity. What about oil and water? Or, test different objects. Place the leads on various objects to see if they conduct electricity. Try a fork, a rubber band, and a potato!

SALTWATER MAGIC

What is the difference between salt water and fresh water?

You certainly wouldn't want to take a giant gulp of salt water! Aside from the taste, there are other differences between the two. Salt water is denser because it contains sodium chloride (that's the salt). This means that salt water is heavier than fresh water. Objects that sink in fresh water can actually float on salt water. Try this project to learn more!

EXPERIMENT #15

MATERIALS

- 2 large wide-mouthed jars, such as Weck jars
- Water
- Measuring cup
- Mixing spoon
- Salt
- 2 eggs

2

3

PROCEDURE

1 Fill two jars with equal amounts of water. It should be deep enough to cover an egg.

2 Pour ½ cup (144 g) of salt into one jar.

3 Stir the saltwater mixture thoroughly.

4 Place an egg in each jar. What happens?

5 Carefully pour fresh water into the saltwater mixture. It works best if you pour the water slowly along the side of the jar. Now what does the egg do?

6 If you are very careful adding the fresh water, you can make it appear as if the egg is hovering in the middle of the jar! Leave it on the counter for an unsuspecting parent to witness the magical hovering egg.

4

6

OBSERVATION

What do you see? If you said the egg in the tap water is sinking but the egg in the salt water is floating, egg-cellent! If for some reason your egg is not floating, remove the egg carefully and add another tablespoon (18 g) of salt. Then place the egg back in the salt water. Once the salt water has enough **density**, the egg will float. If you ever get to swim in the ocean, you'll find floating in the salty water is easier than if you were in a pool, just like the egg in this experiment!

MAKE YER OWN PIRATE TREASURE

How are crystals formed?

Crystals are groups of atoms that are formed in an organized way. Different kinds of crystals have different shapes. They are formed in nature when liquids cool and begin to harden. The molecules gather together in a specific pattern that repeats to result in a crystal.

Some crystals form when magma, a liquid form of rock, cools; when the magma cools slowly, a crystal has time to grow. Some crystals turn into diamonds, rubies, or emeralds. Other kinds of crystal are formed when water evaporates from a saltwater mixture. Salt crystals also form as water evaporates. This is the kind of crystal you will be making here.

MATERIALS

- ❷ 1 medium jar
- ❷ 2 cups (480 ml) water
- ❷ Small saucepan
- ❷ Heatproof measuring cup
- ❷ ¾ cup (225 g) Epsom salt
- ❷ Mixing spoon
- ❷ Food coloring

PROCEDURE

1 Boil the water on the stove. Carefully measure out 1 cup (240 ml) into the heatproof measuring cup, then pour that water into the jar.

2 Stir in ¾ cup (225 g) of Epsom salt. Mix thoroughly. If there is a little salt left at the bottom of the jar, that's okay.

3 Add three to four drops of your favorite color and mix well.

4 Place the jar in the refrigerator. Take a peek every few hours. What's going on in there?

5 After 1 day, observe your crystals. Carefully scrape a large spoon against the bottom of the jar and observe the crystals up close. What do you notice? What shape did the crystals make?

6 Leave the jar in for 2 to 3 more days, then scoop the crystals that have formed. How are they shaped differently?

OBSERVATION

When you take the jar of crystals from your refrigerator, look carefully at it before disturbing it. You probably notice crystals clinging to the sides of the jar. Notice the patterns! At first it may look like there's just a layer of crust along the bottom of the jar. But when you scrape it with the spoon and remove it from the jar, you can see it's much more intricate than a simple crust.

The flat surfaces of the crystals are called facets. They form shapes, such as triangles, rectangles, and squares. Different kinds of crystals are used for different things. Quartz crystals are used in watches. When electricity from a battery buzzes through quartz, it vibrates. These vibrations keep time! Other crystals, such as diamonds, are used for more than just jewelry. Diamonds are so hard they can be used in saws that can cut through other hard rock.

CREATING CLOUDS

How are clouds formed?

Looking up at the sky and watching the clouds can be relaxing. And on a hot day, clouds can cool you off. Dark clouds can make you feel gloomy or nervous if they look like they will bring in a storm.

There are lots of different kinds of clouds in the sky. They have cool superhero names such as cumulonimbus and nimbostratus. What the heck are clouds? You can see them, but you can't feel them! Let's make a cloud first and then explore just what a cloud is.

EXPERIMENT #17

MATERIALS

- ❯ 1 medium jar with lid
- ❯ Ice
- ❯ Hot water
- ❯ Hairspray

PROCEDURE

1 Place the lid of the jar upside down and fill it with ice. Put this off to the side.

2 Heat some water. It doesn't need to be boiling, but it should be hot to the touch. We heated our water to about 120°F (49°C).

3 Carefully pour the hot water into the jar so that it's about 1 inch (2.5 cm) deep. Swirl it around to warm the entire jar.

4 Set the jar down on a hard surface and place the lid filled with ice on top of the jar.

5 Wait 30 seconds.

6 Quickly lift up the lid and spray the hairspray into the jar. Then replace the lid full of ice back on top. Try not to let the warm water vapor escape.

7 A cloud will begin to form. If you have trouble seeing it, put something dark behind the jar. After a minute, remove the lid. The cloud will rise into the air.

OBSERVATION

When you poured the warm water into the jar, some of it turned to water vapor. As it cooled from the icy lid, some of the water vapor **condensed**. This turned some of the water vapor into tiny water droplets. These droplets clung to the particles of hairspray, and presto! A cloud was formed.

The sky is full of water, though you can't see it. Or can you? Remember: Water vapor consists of droplets of water in gas form. When cool, these water droplets can attach to dust, ice, or salt in the air. When enough of these droplets get together, a cloud will form.

Begin observing clouds in nature. Are there areas that seem cloudier than others? Are there more clouds during certain parts of the day?

{ Chapter 4 }

PHYSICAL SCIENCE

Physical science is the study of the inorganic, or nonliving, world. Some scientists say that physical science is the study of matter, or forms of energy. Physical science overlaps with chemistry and earth science as well. This is because the study of theories such as those explaining how the universe was formed (including the Big Bang Theory) is complex and requires different types of scientists to learn and work together.

There are many careers that involve physical science. Sound engineers work at concerts and in recording studios to make sure the audience hears exactly what the performer wants them to hear. Forensic scientists need to know how properties interact if they are investigating a crime scene. You may use physical science when you are trying to decorate your room or create a piece of art.

Physical scientists answer lots of interesting questions. Why do things sound so different if you're underwater? How do we hear sounds? Acoustics, or the study of sounds, is highlighted in the following projects. Physical science also studies how we see things. Optical illusions trick us into thinking we see things that don't exist. Color, light, and patterns are all topics physical scientists explore, and now you will too!

MATERIALS

- 1 widemouthed jar, such as a Weck jar
- Smartphone
- A group of friends
- Paper or plastic cup

TURN UP THE NOISE

How does glass affect sound?

When you get a large group of kids together, you know things can get pretty loud. Sometimes it might be hard to hear. How does sound happen? How does your ear hear it?

Sound is the energy objects make when they vibrate. Oftentimes these vibrations happen so quickly you can't see it happening. These vibrations force air around them to vibrate. When these sound waves reach your ear, they make your ear vibrate as well. We perceive these vibrations as sound.

When sound interacts with a surface, four things can happen. It can reflect off the surface, like a bouncing ball. It also might scatter, be absorbed, or move through the surface. How glass is shaped, how thick or thin it is, and how the glass is created all change its impact on sound. In this experiment, you will learn how sound interacts with glass.

PROCEDURE

1 Play a song from a smartphone or other smallish music-playing device.

2 Lay a glass jar on its side, aiming it toward the direction you'd like the music to travel.

3 Place the phone or device inside the jar.

4 Get your boogie on!

5 Now try placing the device in the paper or plastic cup. Which sounds louder? Which is clearer?

OBSERVATION

Why does glass make an excellent speaker? Because glass is smooth, it won't scatter the sound. And, because of the shape of the jar, it will direct the sound waves directly at you. You'll notice that paper and plastic just don't work as well. This is because they do not transfer the vibrations as well.

→ TRY THIS!

There's another great way to turn up the noise with your jar. If friends are planning a big surprise party in one room and you can't wait to find out what they're planning, use a jar. Turn the open side of the jar against the wall. Place your ear on the bottom of the jar. The sound should magnify so you can hear inside the room!

THE SOUND OF WATER

MATERIALS

> 1 large jar with lid
> Water

The sound of water can be very relaxing. The sounds of water crashing against the shore, rain on the roof, and water fountains trickling are considered soothing by millions of people. Even water in a jar can help people relax. In this experiment, you'll learn how a jar of water can make lots of different, cool sounds.

PROCEDURE

----

1 Fill the jar halfway with water and put the lid on tightly.

2 Hold the jar vertically in one hand and tilt it back and forth. Little tilts allow the water to splash up against the side, keeping the water from hitting the lid. Do you hear anything at all? Now tilt the jar back and forth a little faster. The water will splash against the lid. When the water hits the lid, listen to the high **pitch** of the sound. Watch to see when the actual noise is made: Is it made when the water hits the lid, or when it moves against the lid?

3 Now hold the jar horizontally. The water should be touching both the jar lid and the bottom of the jar. Tap the bottom of the jar with the fleshy part of your pointer finger. Rock the jar back and forth and listen to the difference in sounds. How many different sounds can you make?

OBSERVATION

How many different sounds could you make with just this jar of water? They all happened because the movement of water you heard were the jar to vibrate. The vibrations you heard were sound waves. Some of the noises you made were higher, while others were lower. This is the pitch of the sound. You can use the jar to make a song by changing the position of the jar to change the pitch. If you want to start your own jar science band, grab a group of friends and a variety of jars. Start rockin' out!

→ WHAT IS ASMR?

Different people react differently to sounds. ASMR, or autonomous sensory meridian response, is when you get a tingling or calming sensation in response to hearing different sounds. Not everyone will experience it, but those who do have a physical reaction when they hear certain sounds, such as water in a jar or whispers. ASMR is becoming popular thanks to hundreds of videos online. Millions of people watch them!

A KITCHEN SYMPHONY

How do we hear sound?

We know that sound travels in waves, but how do we hear the difference between sounds? The human ear can detect a wide range of frequencies. You can hear the difference between a grumbly truck and a bird flapping its delicate wings. But how?

There are thousands of tiny hairs inside your ears. These tiny hairs detect different pitches. Hairs at one end of your inner ear detect low frequencies. At the other end are hairs that hear high frequencies. In this experiment, we'll create water jars to play with various pitches. You can learn to make a song!

MATERIALS

- At least 5 jars
- Water
- Spoons for each jar
- Food coloring (optional)

2

4

PROCEDURE

1 Tap your spoon against each empty jar. They should sound the same.

2 Fill the jars with water, making sure each one has a different amount. Make sure one is barely full, one is about half full, and one is mostly full. The rest are up to you!

3 Line up your jars from smallest amount of water to the fullest.

4 If you'd like to, add various colors to the jars. It will make the instruments more fun!

5 Tap your spoon against the jars. How is the sound different in each? Can you make a song?

6 If you'd like a larger variety of sounds, add jars of other sizes. Fill them with various amounts of water. How many different notes can you make?

5

OBSERVATION

When you hit the side of the glass with the spoon, the glass vibrates. When you added the water, the vibrations slowed down slightly. When vibrations move faster, they make a higher pitch. When they move slower, the sound is lower. A jar with more water will have a lower sound. The vibrations are moving slower. Conversely, a jar with less water makes a high sound. This is why the different jars made different sounds.

→ NOTE

The more jars you have, the more notes you can make. We started with five small jars, and then added some medium jars to increase the songs we could play.

→ A SINGING BLACK HOLE

Astronomers have discovered a singing black hole! Researchers are studying how sound waves travel through space. Sound needs something to move through, which is called a medium. This can be air or water, among other things. These scientists are studying whether the gas atoms and dust in outer space can alter sounds coming from galaxies far, far away.

OPTICAL ILLUSIONS

How does light refraction work?

As light travels in one medium, such as air, it travels in a straight line. But, when it has to jump from one medium to another, say air to water, the path of light bends. This is called **refraction**. Refraction is the bending of light as it moves from one transparent substance to another. Refraction is used in eyeglasses, magnifying lenses, and prisms. Magicians also use light refraction to trick an audience.

If you want to blow the minds of your younger siblings or cousins, light refraction is an easy way to do it. Here are a couple things you can do with a simple jar of water.

EXPERIMENT #20

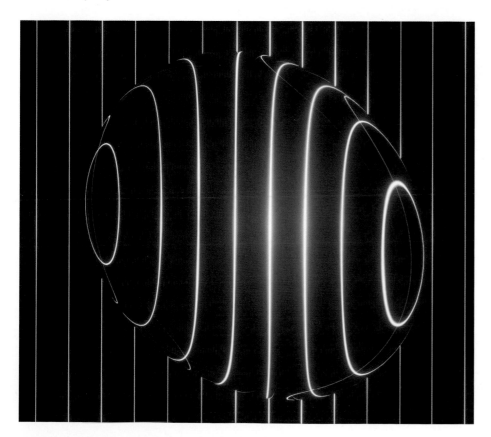

MATERIALS

- 1 small jar
- Water
- Index card
- Marker

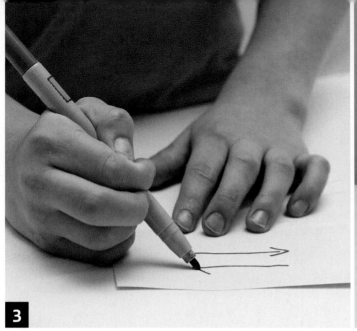

3

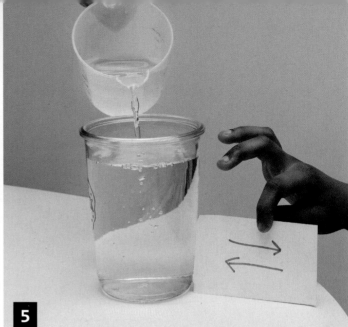

5

PROCEDURE

----

1 Fill the jar with water.

2 Fold the index card in half so that it can stand on a flat surface.

3 On one side of the index card, draw two arrows, one on top of the other, pointing different directions.

4 Bend down to see the jar and index card at eye level.

5 Move the jar of water in front of the index card. What happens to the arrows?

OBSERVATION

The light traveled from the air through the front of the glass jar, and then through the water. It came through the back of the glass jar and back through the air before it hit the picture. This caused the light to refract and make the image appear to reverse. You can try it with letters as well. Try writing some secret codes that require a jar of water to decipher! Or, draw a picture of a waving man. If he waves with one arm, does the arm change when you place the jar of water in front of him?

THE INCREDIBLE BENDING PENCIL

MATERIALS

- ❯ 1 small jar
- ❯ Pencil
- ❯ Water

OBSERVATION

When you put the pencil in the empty jar, nothing happened. But when you put the pencil in the jar of water, the pencil looked like it was in two pieces. This is the magic of light refraction! The pencil appears to bend where the air meets the water. In science terms, this is called the interface. The light traveled from air to water, changing how we see the pencil.

You can even add different liquids to the jar of water and see whether that changes the results. For example, if you add oil to the jar of water and then place the pencil in the jar, does that change what you see?

PROCEDURE

1 Place the pencil in the empty jar. From the side, look to see if the pencil appears straight.

2 Remove the pencil and fill the jar a little over halfway with water.

3 Place the pencil back in the jar and look at it from the side. What do you see now?

4 For an extended trick, move the pencil around the jar. What happens if you place it on the far side of the jar? In the center? To the right of center?

→ MAGIC MONEY

Magicians use light refraction and reflection to do various tricks. Play with water and a coin. Can you make a penny disappear? Here's a hint: Use two jars. Put one penny in the jar, and put one under the jar. Can you figure out the rest?

MATERIALS

- ❯ 5 small jars
- ❯ Water
- ❯ Blue, yellow, and red food coloring
- ❯ 4 white paper towels

IT'S A COLORFUL WORLD

How do we see color?

Imagine a world that only exists in black and white. Hard to do, right? Luckily, the world is a colorful place! But how do we see these vibrant reds and deep blues? It's a combination of physics and biology.

It starts when light falls on an object. Some of the light is absorbed, and some is reflected. We see the reflected light as color. The color is not actually inside the object; it's in the light that shines on the object. Kind of crazy, right? If an object absorbs all the colors except green, it will reflect green and we'll see that color. So really, we see grass as green because the grass is reflecting that color.

The other important factor in seeing color happens in our heads! We see the colors because our eyes have rods and cones. These rods and cones see light and dark, as well as colors. They send information to the brain, which then translates what you see.

This simple project will put your eyes to the test as colors are absorbed and reflected.

PROCEDURE

----

1 Place the jars in a row. Label the jars 1 to 5.

2 Pour water in Jars 1, 3, and 5. Leave Jars 2 and 4 empty.

3 In Jar 1, pour four drops of blue food coloring. In Jar 3, pour four drops of yellow food coloring. In Jar 5, pour four drops of red food coloring.

(CONTINUED)

4 Carefully fold the four white paper towels lengthwise.

5 Place one paper towel from Jar 1 to Jar 2, another from Jar 2 to Jar 3, the third from Jar 3 to Jar 4, and the last one from Jar 4 to Jar 5.

6 Set the jars in a place where you can watch them, but where they won't be disturbed.

7 Watch as the water is absorbed into the paper towels and travels toward the empty jars. If you notice one of the jars of colored water is near empty, you'll want to refill it.

8 Think about other colors. How can you make different shades? Now that you know the steps to the project, can you make purple?

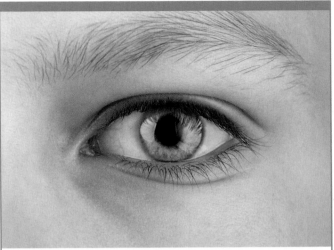

OBSERVATION

Paper towels are made of cellulose fibers. Cellulose is found in wood, cotton, and plants. The key to paper towels' absorption success is the sugar molecules in the cellulose. When water comes into contact with paper towels, the water molecules rush to cling to the paper towels. As you did this experiment, the colorful water was absorbed into the paper towels.

Once each paper towel absorbed as much water as it could handle, it was saturated and could not absorb any more. The colorful water began to slowly fill the empty jar because of this. When both paper towels in the same empty jar were saturated with different colors, the jar was filled with both colors, which mixed to make a new one.

→ ARE YOUR EYES PLAYING TRICKS ON YOU?

Eyes can become tired. This may cause you to see colors that aren't actually there. If you stare at something red for a while and then look at something white, you will see something that is bluish green. Why?

When you look at red, the cones that see red tell your brain that you are seeing red. If you stare at red for a very long time, these cone cells get tired and will not respond for a few minutes. Your cones will only see the other colors until the tired cones wake up!

NAIL SALON SCIENCE

What is surface tension?

Have you ever had the chance to sit quietly near a pond? If so, you may have noticed bugs walking across the water. Or, have you ever noticed that when drops of water fall into a jar of water, the drops make the perfect shape of a circle? This is because of **surface tension**.

You can do some pretty cool art projects using surface tension. For example, you can do some fancy-schmancy nail art! This might take some practice and some patience. Once you get the hang of it, you can create any design you like.

MATERIALS

- 1 medium jar
- Water
- 3 different colors of nail polish, including clear (it works best to use the same brand)
- Toothpicks
- Petroleum jelly
- Cotton swabs

PROCEDURE

1 Fill the jar with water so it is almost full.

2 Hover the first color of nail polish over the water. Let it slowly drip onto the surface of the water. Don't break the surface! The color will expand and float on top of the water.

3 Hover the second color over the water and first color. Let it gently drop onto the surface.

4 Using a cotton swab, smooth petroleum jelly over the skin around your nail edges, but not the nail itself! This will keep the nail polish from sticking to your skin.

(CONTINUED)

5 Very gently, take a toothpick and drag it along the surface of the nail polish colors. The colors will swirl. This may take a few attempts!

6 Dip your finger into the nail polish mixture. Your finger can break the surface of the water and the nail polish will wrap around your finger. Because of this, try not to dip your whole finger into the jar!

7 Repeat with each nail you would like painted.

8 Carefully wipe the petroleum jelly off of your skin. It should come off easily.

9 Let your nails dry for about 5 minutes, then add a top clear coat to protect those fancy nails!

OBSERVATION

Surface tension is when a force in a liquid acts as an elastic sheet. It happens because particles at the surface of the liquid are pulled toward the rest of the liquid. The molecules at the surface of a glass of water cling to the water molecules below them. A needle resting at the surface of a jar of water will stay on its surface. Once it breaks the surface tension, though, it will sink.

When you placed the nail polish on the top of the water, the nail polish rested on top of the water. When you dragged the toothpick along the water to mix the colors, they continued to rest on top of the water (unless you broke the surface of the water). In some cases, the nail polish may have clung to the toothpick. If the toothpick or nail polish broke the surface of the water, you saw the colors sink—which actually is a cool experiment too!

Try dropping the nail polish directly into the water, hard enough to break the surface. Molecules in the nail polish will cling together, creating a gooey, blobby ooze floating around the water.

MATERIALS

- ❯ 1 small jar with lid
- ❯ 2 strong magnets
- ❯ Tape
- ❯ Iron filings

MAGNET MAYHEM

How do magnets work?

At one time, magnets must have been mysterious. There are a lot of stories about how they were discovered: 4,000 years ago, a shepherd in Greece discovered a rock after his shoe was stuck to it. In ancient Rome, a magic stone attracted iron. And in Scandinavia in 1000 AD, Vikings used magnetized needles to determine north and south. This is one of the first known compasses, which use magnets.

Magnets can be fun to play with. After all, they pull things, they push things, and they can attract other magnets. So how do they work? Let's do an experiment or two and find out.

PROCEDURE

1 Determine the north and south poles of the magnets. The north side of the first magnet will be attracted to the south side of the second magnet.

2 Tape the magnets to opposite sides of the outside of the jar. Make sure opposite sides of the magnet are facing each other (south to north).

3 Pour iron filings into the jar and close the lid.

4 Turn the jar on its side, rolling it slowly so the iron filings stick to the magnets.

5 When you spin the jar, observe how the iron pieces move.

6 Continue to spin the jar slowly, attempting to get every filing connected to the magnets.

OBSERVATION

There are two places on Earth that contain magnetic poles: the North Magnetic Pole and the South Magnetic Pole. These are not the same as the geographic north and south poles, though. Instead, they are **magnetic fields**. Every magnet is surrounded by a magnetic field. Mathematicians refer to this as a vector field. This magnetic field is the magnetic force in the space of something magnetic.

Magnets have a north pole and a south pole. The north pole of one magnet is attracted to the south pole of another magnet.

MAGNETS IN WATER

MATERIALS

- ❯ 1 small jar
- ❯ Water
- ❯ Iron filings
- ❯ Magnets (the stronger the better)

OBSERVATION

When you dragged the magnet along the iron filings, the iron filings followed. It turns out that the magnetic field still works under water! If you still haven't had enough fun, try using different liquids. Will using salt water or oil affect the magnetic properties?

Another fun way to play with magnets, and even get a better look at the magnetic field, is to play with magnets and water.

PROCEDURE

1 Place 2 tablespoons (10 g) of iron filings into the jar.

2 Fill the jar about three-quarters full with water.

3 Place the magnet along the side of the jar. Do the iron filings follow?

4 Allow 5 minutes to pass. Shake up the iron filings a bit. Does the magnet have a stronger impact once the filings have been submerged for a length of time?

➜ IS THE EARTH ONE BIG MAGNET?

Why yes, yes it is. Deep in the center, the planet is liquid iron, nickel, and other metals. It gooshes and splooshes around. As the liquid metals move, they create electric currents, which produce magnetic fields. Pretty cool, eh?

SPACE EXPLORATION

How do satellites get launched into outer space?

A satellite is an object that orbits a planet or star. Earth is a satellite because it orbits the sun. The moon is a satellite too. But we usually think of satellites as manmade objects that we send into space. Satellites can't just be catapulted into space like a baseball. They would fall back down to Earth. Let's try a simple experiment to see whether you can figure out how satellites are launched into orbit.

MATERIALS

- 1 medium jar
- About 4 feet (1.2 m) of string
- 1 washer or nut of any size
- Tape
- A surface for the washer to hang above the glass (see step 1)

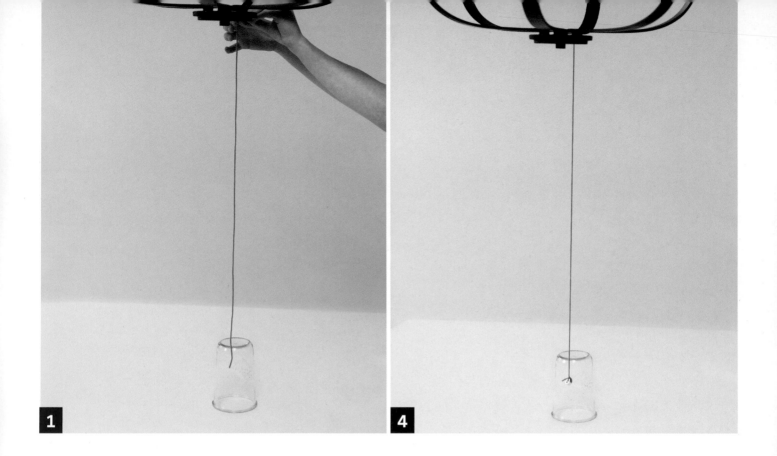

PROCEDURE

1. In this experiment, the string will need to be attached to a stable surface, such as a cabinet or even the bottom of a kitchen table. The jar will be directly underneath it. Cut the string so that it can hang from the surface to just past the jar.

2. Tie the metal washer to one end of the string. The washer will be the satellite.

3. Tape the other end of the string to the hard surface.

4. Place the jar upside down directly under the hanging washer. The washer will angle off the side of the jar.

5. Now it's time to launch your satellite. Can you move the washer so that it orbits around the jar without hitting it? Part of being a scientist is trying different methods. It's okay if it takes a few tries. If you need the trick, see step 6.

6. Did you swing it to the side and push it? If so, it likely just hit the jar. If you swung as hard as you could, it may have jerked the string and hit the jar. Instead, swing the washer parallel to the jar so that it is pushed sideways from the jar. Satellites actually need to be launched sideways!

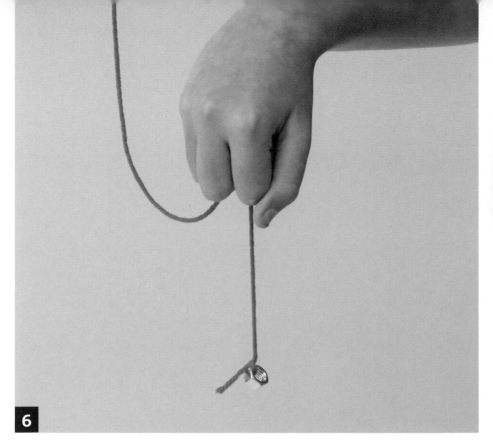

6

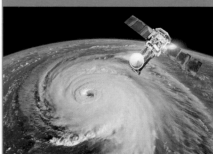

→ **SATELLITES IN ACTION**

Some satellites take pictures of hurricanes or other large weather patterns that help meteorologists. Others take pictures of other galaxies far, far away. Many satellites are used for communication or beam television signals so we can see our favorite TV shows on Earth.

OBSERVATION

If the satellite goes too fast, it will fly away. However, if it goes too slow, the satellite will fall to Earth. Satellites need to go just the right **orbital velocity** so that they stay in space, following the Earth's orbit. And, satellites need to be just the right distance away from the Earth. If a satellite is too low, it can burn up in the atmosphere. Rockets help satellites by carrying them into space. The rockets are launched with the satellite attached. Once the rocket is the right elevation above Earth's atmosphere, it will start heading sideways. It can reach speeds up to 18,000 miles (28,968 km) an hour. Once the rocket has reached the correct height and speed, it will release the satellite. The satellite will continue to orbit Earth on its own, sending a variety of information to Earth.

Chapter 5

ENVIRONMENTAL SCIENCE

Environmental scientists study ecology, geology, biology, meteorology, chemistry, physics, or engineering. Their research helps us understand how our planet is changing and how our actions may help or hurt the land, water, and air around us.

Their research can also change how politicians make laws. For example, they may take samples of water near large factories in order to measure the level of nutrients or chemicals in the water. If large amounts of dangerous chemicals are discovered in the water, the government may use that information to make new laws about how factories handle chemicals so as not to impact the water.

Several companies hire environmental scientists to help them from accidentally harming the soil, water, or air. Governments hire environmental scientists to learn how oceans are changing. They may also research new ways of harvesting wind to better use wind energy to power televisions or computers.

When an oil tanker spilled 42 million liters of oil into the ocean, environmental scientists were called to help the cleanup effort for the water and shorelines. Decades later, they still study how that oil spill directly impacted land and animals.

One thing all environmental scientists have in common is that they care about the planet and the plants and animals living on it, and they are doing their best to make the planet better in years to come.

MATERIALS

- 2 large jars
- Fruit and vegetable scraps
- Leaves, grass clippings, and sticks or twigs
- Water
- Soil or potting mix
- Measuring cup
- Fabric squares (an old T-shirt cut into squares works well)
- Rubber bands

ALL ABOUT COMPOST

Does soil help decomposition?

If compost is basically garbage, you may wonder why it matters whether it's tossed into a garbage bag or composted. When trash is tossed into the garbage, it goes to a landfill. Often this trash will be put underground, where it will lack the opportunity to mix with oxygen. It will create methane, a gas that contributes to climate change. If compostable material stays above ground, it mixes with oxygen and breaks down to add nutrients to soil.

When creating a compost pile, it helps to have a mix of materials that create both carbon and nitrogen. Things that create carbon include fruit waste, newspapers, and sticks. Things that create nitrogen include coffee grounds, vegetable scraps, and grass clippings.

The key to composting is the decomposition of materials. This is how materials break down so nutrients can return to the planet. Okay, so we know composting helps the planet. But what is the best way to compost? We'll explore that in this project.

PROCEDURE

1 In each jar, place the same amount of vegetable and fruit scraps.

2 Into each container, place the same amount of leaves, grass clippings, and sticks.

3 In each container, pour about ¼ cup (60 ml) of water. Too much water may cause a lack of oxygen. If this happens, the mixture may begin to smell really bad. If that happens, either try the experiment again with less water or pour some water out to see if that helps. The jar only needs to be damp.

4 To one jar, add a cup of soil or potting mix. Don't add any to the other jar.

(CONTINUED)

5 Seal the jars by placing the fabric squares over the jar openings and securing with rubber bands.

6 Place both jars in a place where they will be undisturbed but where they can be observed each day. A well-ventilated area, such as outside, will work well as long as it is kept away from critters that may be attracted to rotting food!

7 This project may take several weeks, maybe even a month, to really see the difference! When you are finished, you can add it to a compost bin. See page 111 to learn how to build your own!

OBSERVATION

In the beginning, your compost jar may be very pretty! Look at the beautiful colors of the fruits and vegetables. Over time, though, it will break down and be a lot less pretty. As the food decomposes, it is releasing nutrients into the soil. After you've observed your compost jar, add it to the soil outside. Mix it in with the existing soil to fertilize the ground.

You should notice the jar with the potting soil decomposed faster. Soil is rich with microbes, which speed up the process and help keep insects away from your other composted material.

BUILD AN INDOOR COMPOSTING BIN

MATERIALS

- 1 large container, about 8 inches (20 cm) deep, with lid
- Bedding: shredded or corrugated cardboard is best (peat moss can work, and so can shredded newspapers, but they must be kept damp)
- Water
- Red wiggler worms, tiger worms, or manure worms (see Resources, page 125)
- Coffee grounds, fruit or vegetable scraps, or leaves

If you don't have a large yard, you can build an indoor composting bin. There are some materials you should not include in your indoor compost. This includes breads, cooking oils, diseased plants, meat, and coated paper such as magazines or postcards. These can make your compost smell bad, and they aren't going to help the soil gain nutrients either.

PROCEDURE

1 Place the bedding in the bin.

2 Pour water over the bedding so that it becomes saturated but not soaked. The bedding needs to absorb the water, so leave this be for up to a day. The end result should be bedding that is moist, not wet.

3 Add the worms, then add the kitchen scraps.

4 After about 3 to 4 months, the compost should be ready to add to the soil outside.

Tip: You should clean the worm poop, called castings, if you plan to keep your compost bin permanently. One way to do this is to remove some of the compost and add new, damp bedding and scraps.

→ FARMING COMPOST

Rather than allow food to go to waste in New York City, enormous compost farms are being built about 60 miles (97 km) away. Imagine all of the table scraps and waste being used to fertilize plants instead of taking up room in landfills!

MATERIALS

- 3 small jars
- Water
- 3 candy-coated chocolates

CANDY EROSION

What is erosion, and how does it affect the planet?

Our planet is made of many landforms. Some of these landforms include steep mountains and valleys. Other places have gently rolling hills. Still other places are flat as far as the eye can see. But all of these landforms have things in common. They are changed because of erosion. Erosion is a geological process in which the Earth is worn down because of wind or water.

Wind erosion happens where soil is dry and loose. Different types of soil erode faster or slower than others. Wind erosion can have a dangerous result because it can take nutrients away from plants.

Water erosion is different. There are many kinds of water erosion, but rain is a simple example. Raindrops can break apart soil structures and lead to landslides.

Valley erosion happens when water moves continuously against a surface. Think of a river flowing against rocks. The water may not seem strong, but if it keeps moving, it gradually wears away at the hard surface. Fast-moving water will make more impressive cuts to the rock. Valleys are created this way. This simple (yet delicious) experiment will show how continuous water erodes hard surfaces.

PROCEDURE

1 Label three jars 1, 2, and 3.

2 Fill the jars about halfway with water.

3 Place a candy in each of the three jars.

4 Swirl Jar 1 for about 30 seconds, then let it rest for a minute. Swirl it again, and then leave it undisturbed again.

5 Vigorously shake Jar 2 as much as you can for 5 minutes. If you need to take a break, see whether you can get an assistant!

6 Leave Jar 3 untouched.

7 At the end of 5 minutes, observe the differences between the candies.

OBSERVATION

What happens to the candies? Which one eroded faster? Remember, water will have an immediate impact on the surface of some objects. You likely noticed that the color coating came off of the candy as soon as it came in contact with water. The candy that was left alone, however, had its color last longer. The jar that was gently swirled lost the color coating faster but still remained coated with the hard candy shell. The candy that was shaken vigorously probably became a small piece of chocolate fairly quickly. It was the first to show signs of erosion. This is because the faster water is moving, the greater the erosion.

If you'd like to try a more delicious version of this experiment, place one of the chocolate candies in your mouth. But don't bite it! Just leave it on your tongue. Does the chocolate coating erode even faster?

→ HOW TO HELP

One way to prevent water erosion is by planting **vegetation**. Vegetation slows down water as it travels. This way water has more time to soak into the ground. This helps keep nutrients in the ground, where it can help the ecosystem thrive.

IT'S TOO HOT UP HERE

What is convection?

On a hot summer night, do you prefer to sleep downstairs? If so, you already know about **convection**. Convection is the transfer of heated molecules through air or liquid. When the molecules move, they take the heat with them. As air is heated, it expands and rises. Cool air takes the place of the hot air that has risen. This is why the upper level in a two-story house tends to be warmer. Find out more in these experiments!

To learn how temperatures behave differently, we can use jars of hot and cold water.

MATERIALS

- ❯ 2 medium jars
- ❯ Bowl big enough to hold 1 jar
- ❯ Ice
- ❯ Water (both hot and cold water)
- ❯ Blue and red food coloring

PROCEDURE

1 Fill the bowl with ice.

2 Fill the first jar with cold water and settle it inside the ice. Let it sit for about 5 minutes.

3 Fill the second jar with water as hot as you can stand it. It doesn't have to be boiling, but it does need to be hot.

4 Take the jar out of the ice water and place the two jars side by side.

5 Pour three drops of red food coloring in the jar of hot water. Pour three drops of blue food coloring in the jar of cold water. What happens in each jar? How is it different?

OBSERVATIONS

The red food coloring should have diffused, or spread through the jar of water, faster than the blue. This is because hot water has more energy than cold water. This means the molecules in hot water move faster.

COLORFUL CURRENTS

MATERIALS

- 1 small jar
- Water
- Freezer
- 1 microwave-safe mug or glass
- Microwave
- Food coloring
- Spoon
- Dropper

OBSERVATION

The hot water rose and then spread across the surface of the cold water. This is because the hot water had more kinetic energy than the cold water. The hot molecules pushed apart, lowering the density of the hot water, allowing it to float. Over time, the temperature evened out. The word for this is convection current. It eventually turned all of the water the color you chose.

PROCEDURE

1 Fill the jar halfway with water.

2 Place the jar in the freezer for about 10 minutes. Don't let the water freeze!

3 Fill the microwave-safe container about half full of water and microwave for about 20 seconds.

4 Add 5 drops of food coloring to the hot water and mix.

5 Remove the jar from the freezer and place it on the table. Wait for the water to become still.

6 Fill the dropper with hot, colored water.

7 Lower the dropper of hot water into the cold water until the tip of the dropper is near the bottom.

8 Gently release some of the colored water. Observe what happens.

9 Release more of the colored water along the bottom of the cold jar. What do you see?

MATERIALS

- 4 small jars
- Water
- Salt
- Vinegar
- Cooking oil
- 4 iron nails (or other pieces of iron)

THE GREAT RUST RACE

Why can't I leave my bike out in the rain?

Everything on our planet is made of atoms. These atoms are constantly in motion, and when they come together or move apart, a new substance is created. This chemical reaction causes new properties. Rust is an example of a metal, usually iron, reacting with oxygen. Rust happens if water is present.

Iron rusts very quickly. It only takes a few hours for iron to rust if it is exposed to air and water. After this experiment, you'll understand why iron may not be the best metal to work with. It will corrode quickly. This means the metal, which is actually quite strong, can break down and fall apart.

While it might not seem like a big deal, corrosion can have a negative impact on the environment. Rusted pipes can cause gasses or liquids to leak into the environment. Producing new materials (even that bike!) requires factory work, which will cause **pollution**. Let's do the experiment first, then learn how to prevent rust from building.

PROCEDURE

1 Prepare each jar. Fill the first jar with just water. Fill the second jar with water and add 1 tablespoon (18 g) of salt. Fill the third jar with vinegar and the fourth jar with cooking oil.

2 Place one nail in each jar.

3 Check on the jars each day and record your observations. Which one starts to rust first? After 2 weeks, which nail is rustiest?

OBSERVATION

As you read, iron will rust when exposed to air and water. The rust you see is iron oxide, the result of oxygen molecules combing with the dissolving iron. The rust is a new compound. So how do we prevent rust? Iron cannot rust if there is no water, so keeping iron dry will prevent rust from happening. Other materials prevent rust. Stainless steel, especially if it is mixed with nickel, will not rust easily. Spraying a metal with acrylic or polyester powder will protect it once heat has been applied.

EXPERIMENT #29

DON'T BE A LITTERBUG

What impact does litter have on our water?

Our planet has a finite amount of water. All the water we have is all the water we will ever have, so it is important to take care of it. Keeping our water clean is a responsibility we have to future generations. Unfortunately, pollution is having a negative impact on our water. Pollution is the introduction of something harmful or poisonous into the environment. While some pollution can be cleaned, not all of it can. Let's do an experiment to learn more about the impact of pollution in our waterways.

MATERIALS

- ❯ 3 jars with lids
- ❯ Marker
- ❯ Water
- ❯ Laundry detergent
- ❯ Plastic toys
- ❯ Paper
- ❯ 3 spoons

PROCEDURE

----

1 Fill each jar about three-quarters full with water.

2 In the first jar, add ¼ cup (60 ml) of laundry detergent. Shred some pieces of paper and add them to the second jar. Place some plastic toys in the third jar.

3 Place the lids on the jars and shake them vigorously.

4 Using the spoons, try to remove the pollutants from each jar. How easy is it to move each object? Are some easier to remove than others?

OBSERVATION

Some of the objects were easier to clean up than others. You could easily scoop the plastic toys, as well as most of the paper. The detergent was likely quite a challenge! Litter, such as paper and bags, is pretty easy to scoop out of the water. But what if no one cleans it up? What happens if a fish gets trapped in a snack bag or an animal tries to eat litter? It was easy to clean most of the paper, wasn't it? That's why it's so important for us to clean up after ourselves.

While the plastic toys were probably easy to scoop up, they can still do great harm to the water system. There are a few reasons why. First, wildlife can get trapped in plastic pieces, such as grocery bags or netting. Second, as plastic breaks down, it leaks dangerous chemicals into the waterways and soil. These toxins, though they may be invisible, can harm and even kill wildlife. Third, plastic can break down into even tinier pieces of plastic, which can also be poisonous to animals. While some plastic can be recycled, much of it can't or isn't. One way you can help is to use reusable water bottles or bags whenever possible.

→ DETERGENT IN THE WRONG WATER

Detergent may make your laundry clean when it mixes with water in the washing machine. But a large amount of detergent in our water system is deadly. It can wear away the layer of skin that protects fish from bacteria and parasites. Detergent can also damage fish gills, not to mention kill fish eggs. As if that weren't bad enough, detergents can lead to algae blooms that poison waterways. Until scientists find a way to solve the problem, environmentalists encourage people to choose eco-friendly detergents that still clean clothes but are safer for the environment.

Think of all the liquids that are so toxic they cannot be poured down a sink. Chemicals such as oil and antifreeze are necessary in our cars and lawn mowers, but they are bad for the planet. Disposing of them correctly, by taking them to a recycling center, is an extremely important part of using technology responsibly.

GLOSSARY

Acid: A chemical with a lot of hydrogen ions, measuring 0 to 7 on the pH scale.

Aerate: To move air into a substance.

Air pressure: The force exerted onto a surface by the weight of the air.

Atom: The basic unit of an element.

Base: A chemical with a lot of hydroxide ions, measuring 7 to 14 on the pH scale.

Compound: A substance made of two or more separate elements.

Condense: To change from a gas state to a liquid state, or liquid state to a solid state.

Conductor: A material that conducts heat, electricity, light, or sound.

Control: The constant against which other parts of an experiment will be compared.

Convection: The transfer of heat when hot air rises, causing cold air to sink.

Density: The measurement of mass per unit of volume. The density of an object is its mass divided by its volume.

Electric current: The flow of an electric charge.

Erosion: The slow wearing away of something.

Evaporate: To change from a liquid state to a gas.

Hypothesis: An educated guess or explanation based on limited information. A hypothesis is the starting point for conducting research.

Magnetic field: A region within the force of magnetism.

Monomer: Unconnected molecules that can bond together to create chains of polymers.

Orbital velocity: The speed at which a body revolves around another body.

Pitch: The quality of determining sound as high or low.

Pollution: The introduction of a harmful or poisonous substance into an environment.

Polymer: A substance with similar units bonded together.

Producer: An organism, either a green plant or bacterium, that is the first level of the food chain. It can use energy from the sun to make its own food.

Proton: A particle with a positive charge.

Refraction: The phenomenon of waves passing through one medium to another.

Scientific method: An organized system for conducting research.

Surface tension: The tension of a surface caused by attraction of particles at the surface layer.

Transpiration: The process in which plants absorb water and then give off water vapor.

Vegetation: Plants.

Vortex: A mass of whirling fluid or air.

RESOURCES

Now that you're a scientist, don't stop experimenting! Create your own projects, and check out the following books for inspiration. All of them provide fun, engaging activities that will promote both science and art.

Robinson, Tom. *The Everything Kids' Science Experiments Book.* October 2001.

Chatterton, Crystal. *Awesome Science Experiments for Kids: 100+Fun STEM/STEAM Projects and Why They Work.* 2018.

Carey, Anne. *STEAM Kids: 50+ Science/Technology/ Engineering/Art/Math Hands-On Projects for Kids.* September 2016.

Heinecki, Liz Lee. *STEAM Lab for Kids: 52 Creative Hands-On Projects for Exploring Science, Technology, Engineering, Art, and Math.* May 2018.

Graves, Colleen, and Aaron Graves. *The Big Book of Maker Space Projects.* 2017.

The following websites provide scientists with a variety of projects. They also explain how and why they work!

Science Buddies
www.sciencebuddies.org/science-fair-projects/project-ideas

Education.com
www.education.com/science-fair/

The National Energy Education Development Project
www.need.org/sciencefair

WORKS CITED

Chapter 1

Science Buddies. "Snuggly Science: How Puppies Keep Warm." *Scientific American.* www.scientificamerican.com/article/bring-science-home-huddling-puppies/

Great Lakes Lessons. "Food Chains and Webs." Michigan Sea Grant. www.miseagrant.umich.edu/lessons/lessons/by-broad-concept/life-science/food-chains-and-webs/

"Group Sleeping Huddling." Mouse Ethogram, Stanford School of Medicine. web.stanford.edu/~jeromeg/cgi-bin/Group%20 sleeping%20-%20Huddling.php

Johnson, Sarah. "Earthworms Are More Important than Pandas (If You Want to Save the Planet)." The Conversation. theconversation.com/earthworms-are-more-important-than-pandas-if-you-want-to-save-the-planet-74010

"Pond Water Critters Protozoan Guide." Microbus Microscope Educational Website. microscope-microscope.org/pond-water-critters-protozoan-guide/

Robb, Graham. "The Big Sleep." *New York Times.* www.nytimes.com/2007/11/25/opinion/25robb.html

Spector, Dina. "Here's How Many Days a Person Can Survive without Water." *Business Insider.* www.businessinsider.com/how-many-days-can-you-survive-without-water-2014-5

University of Queensland. "Ancient mice discovered by climate cavers." ScienceDaily. www.sciencedaily.com/releases/2018/09/180924185050.htm

Van Egmond, Wim, and Dave Walker. "A Simple Guide to Small and Microscopic Pond Life." *Micscape Microscopy and Microscope Magazine.* www.microscopy-uk.org.uk/pond/x_index.html

Chapter 2

Mac, Ryan. "How Do Acids & Bases Affect Our Daily Lives?" Sciencing.com. sciencing.com/do-bases-affect-daily-lives-6460548.html

Rohrig, Brian. "The Science of Slime!" American Chemical Society. www.acs.org/content/dam/acsorg/education/resources/highschool/chemmatters/articlesbytopic/solidsliquidsgases/chemmatters-dec2004-slime.pdf

Chapter 3

"Condensation." National Geographic Society. www.nationalgeographic.org/encyclopedia/condensation/

"Condensation - The Water Cycle." Adhesion and Cohesion Water Properties, The USGS Water Science School. water.usgs.gov/edu/watercyclecondensation.html

"Conductivity Meter." Exploratorium: The Museum of Science, Art and Human Perception, Exploratorium Teacher Institute. www.exploratorium.edu/snacks/conductivity-meter

Greene, Brian. "How Did Water Come to Earth?" *Smithsonian Magazine.* www.smithsonianmag.com/science-nature/how-did-water-come-to-earth-72037248/

Hitt, David. "What Are Clouds?" NASA Knows! (Grades K–4) Series. www.nasa.gov/audience/forstudents/k-4/stories/nasa-knows/what-are-clouds-k4.html

"How Do Crystals Form & Grow?" Geology Page. www.geologypage.com/2016/03/how-do-crystals-form-grow.html

"How to Measure Tornadoes: The EF Scale." *Old Farmer's Almanac,* Yankee Publishing Inc. www.almanac.com/content/how-measure-tornadoes-ef-scale

Huds, Dirk. "What Animals Live in the Bathyal Zone?" Sciencing.com, sciencing.com/animals-live-bathyal-zone-6746859.html

Kellum, Jacki. "Ocean Zones and Who Live There." Ocean Worlds. oceanworlds.wordpress.com/2015/06/25/ocean-zones-and-animals-who-live-there

Powell, Jack. "Four Biggest Differences Between the Ocean & Fresh Water." Sciencing.com, sciencing.com/four-between-ocean-fresh-water-8519973.html

Robert, Chuck. "Why Is Condensation Important?" Sciencing.com, sciencing.com/condensation-important-10016936.html

Wicker, Crystal. "Tornadoes." Weather Wiz Kids Weather Information for Kids. www.weatherwizkids.com/weather-tornado.htm

Woodford, Chris. "How Quartz Watches and Clocks Work." Explain That Stuff. www.explainthatstuff.com/quartzclockwatch.html

Chapter 4

Ault, Alicia. "Ask Smithsonian: How Does a Satellite Stay Up?" *Smithsonian Magazine.* www.smithsonianmag.com/smithsonian-institution/ask-smithsonian-how-does-satellite-stay-180954165

Chudler, Eric H. "The Retina." Neuroscience for Kids, University of Washington. faculty.washington.edu/chudler/retina.html

Danit, Brown. "How Do Paper Towels Absorb Water?" Indiana Public Media, Moment of Science. indianapublicmedia.org/amomentofscience/how-do-paper-towels-absorb-water

"Interpreting the 'Song' Of a Distant Black Hole." NASA's Goddard Space Flight Center. www.nasa.gov/centers/goddard/universe/black_hole_sound.html

"Planet Earth: A Great Magnet." Space Weather Center. www.spaceweathercenter.org/swop/Science_Briefs/Magnet/1.html.

Stillman, Dan. "What Is a Satellite?" NASA Knows! (Grades 5–8) Series. www.nasa.gov/audience/forstudents/5-8/features/nasa-knows/what-is-a-satellite-58.html

"What Causes the Earth's Magnetic Field?" Institute of Physics. www.physics.org/article-questions.asp?id=64

Woodford, Chris. "Sound - The Science of Waves, How They Travel, How We Use Them." Explain That Stuff. www.explainthatstuff.com/sound.html

Chapter 5

"About Corrosion and the Environment." Lehigh University, www.lehigh.edu/~amb4/wbi/kwardlow/corrosion.htm

"Causes of Water Erosion." Erosion Pollution, GEI Works. www.erosionpollution.com/water-erosion.html

"Detergents Occurring in Freshwater." Lenntech. www.lenntech.com/aquatic/detergents.htm

"Environmental Scientists and Specialists - What Do They Do?" StudentScholarships.org. studentscholarships.org/salary/370/environmental_scientists_and_specialists.php#sthash.gON3JlvK.dpbs

Graham, Sarah. "Environmental Effects of Exxon Valdez Spill Still Being Felt." Scientific American. www.scientificamerican.com/article/environmental-effects-of

"Heat Convection in Liquids." Education.com. www.education.com/science-fair/article/convection-movement-heat-fluids

"How to Prevent Rust." Metal Supermarkets. www.metalsupermarkets.com/how-to-prevent-rust

Maldarelli, Claire. "Anyone Can Compost Their Food Waste (and Everyone Should)." Popular Science. www.popsci.com/how-to-compost#page-2

"Wind Erosion." The National Soil Erosion Research Laboratory, Purdue University. milford.nserl.purdue.edu/weppdocs/overview/wndersn.html

ƒ BOUT THE AUTHOR

Julia Garstecki received her bachelor's degree from Michigan State University (go green!) and her master's degree from SUNY Fredonia. Julia has been teaching for over 20 years. Currently she teaches at Goodwin College in East Hartford, Connecticut. She has published dozens of nonfiction books for intermediate and hi-lo readers, including *Pick, Spit & Scratch: The Science of Disgusting Habits* and *Burp, Spit & Fart: The Science Behind Gross Things Babies Do*. For more about Julia (and pictures of her toy poodle, Bella), visit her website at juliagarstecki.com.

ƒ CKNOWLEDGMENTS

I am eternally grateful for the patience of my two children, who not only helped refine the projects developed for this book, but agreed to model as well. I'm also grateful for my husband, who never complained about the jars and various materials piled on the dining room table, or about the experiments in various stages scattered around the house for almost a year while the book was in progress.

ABOUT THE PHOTOGRAPHERS

Best friends and colleagues since 2010, Rebecca Wilhite and Mary Swank are the photography duo that make up Rebecca Wilhite Photography in Hartford, Connecticut. Rebecca and Mary reside with their husbands, Scott and Jeff, respectively, and would like to thank them for their unending support. Learn more at rebeccawilhitephotography.com.

INDEX